Vernon Lee

Renaissance Fancies and Studies

Being a sequel to Euphorion

Vernon Lee

Renaissance Fancies and Studies
Being a sequel to Euphorion

ISBN/EAN: 9783744790543

Printed in Europe, USA, Canada, Australia, Japan

Cover: Foto ©ninafisch / pixelio.de

More available books at **www.hansebooks.com**

SMITH, ELDER, & CO.'S PUBLICATIONS.

THE LIFE OF SIR JAMES FITZJAMES STEPHEN, Bart., K.C.S.I., a Judge of the High Court of Justice. By his Brother, LESLIE STEPHEN. Second Edition. With 2 Portraits. Demy 8vo, 16s.

AN AGNOSTIC'S APOLOGY; and other Essays. By LESLIE STEPHEN. Large crown 8vo, 10s. 6d.

LIFE OF HENRY FAWCETT. By LESLIE STEPHEN. With 2 Steel Portraits. Fifth Edition. Large crown 8vo, 12s. 6d.

HOURS IN A LIBRARY. By LESLIE STEPHEN. Revised, Rearranged, and Cheaper Edition, with additional Chapters. 3 vols. crown 8vo, 6s. each.

A HISTORY OF ENGLISH THOUGHT IN THE EIGHTEENTH CENTURY. Second Edition. By LESLIE STEPHEN. 2 vols. demy 8vo, 28s.

THE SCIENCE OF ETHICS: an Essay upon Ethical Theory, as Modified by the Doctrine of Evolution. By LESLIE STEPHEN. Demy 8vo, 16s.

LIFE OF FRANK BUCKLAND. By his Brother-in-Law, GEORGE C. BOMPAS, Editor of "Notes and Jottings from Animal Life." With a Portrait. Crown 8vo, 5s.; gilt edges, 6s.

RENAISSANCE IN ITALY. By JOHN ADDINGTON SYMONDS. THE REVIVAL OF LEARNING. Second Edition. Demy 8vo, 16s. THE FINE ARTS. Second Edition. Demy 8vo, 16s. THE CATHOLIC REACTION. 2 vols. demy 8vo, 32s.

SHAKSPERE'S PREDECESSORS IN THE ENGLISH DRAMA. By JOHN ADDINGTON SYMONDS. Demy 8vo, 16s.

AN ARTIST'S REMINISCENCES. By RUDOLPH LEHMANN. With Portrait. Demy 8vo, 12s. 6d. net.

A SHORT HISTORY OF THE RENAISSANCE IN ITALY. Taken from the work of JOHN ADDINGTON SYMONDS. By Lieut.-Col. ALFRED PEARSON. With a Steel Engraving of a recent Portrait of Mr. Symonds. Demy 8vo, 12s. 6d.

VOLTAIRE'S VISIT TO ENGLAND, 1726-1729. By ARCHIBALD BALLANTYNE. Crown 8vo, 8s. 6d.

THE JOCKEY CLUB AND ITS FOUNDERS. By ROBERT BLACK, M.A., Author of "Horse Racing in France," &c. Crown 8vo, 10s. 6d.

THE LIFE AND LETTERS OF ROBERT BROWNING. By Mrs. SUTHERLAND ORR. With Portrait, and Steel Engraving of Mr. Browning's Study in De Vere Gardens. Second Edition. Crown 8vo, 12s. 6d.

LIBERTY, EQUALITY, FRATERNITY. By Sir JAMES FITZJAMES STEPHEN, K.C.S.I. Second Edition, with a new Preface. Demy 8vo, 14s.

LIFE AND WRITINGS OF JOSEPH MAZZINI. In 6 vols. crown 8vo, 4s. 6d. each.

EXTRACTS FROM THE WRITINGS OF W. M. THACKERAY. Chiefly Philosophical and Reflective. Cheap Edition. Fcap. 8vo, 2s. 6d.

HISTORY OF ART. By Dr. WILHELM LÜBKE. Translated by F. E. BUNNETT. With 415 Illustrations. Third Edition. 2 vols. imp. 8vo, 42s.

WALKS IN FLORENCE AND ITS ENVIRONS. By SUSAN and JOANNA HORNER. With numerous Illustrations. 2 vols. crown 8vo, 15s.

London: SMITH, ELDER, & CO., 15 Waterloo Place.

SMITH, ELDER, & CO.'S PUBLICATIONS.

OUR SQUARE AND CIRCLE; or, the Annals of a Little London House. By "JACK EASEL," sometime *Punch's* Roving Correspondent. With a Frontispiece. Crown 8vo, 5s.

GERALD EVERSLEY'S FRIENDSHIP: A Study in Real Life. By the Rev. J. E. C. WELLDON, Head Master of Harrow School. Third Edition. Crown 8vo, 6s.

OFF THE MILL. By the Right Rev. G. F. BROWNE, D.C.L., Bishop of Stepney. With 2 Illustrations. Crown 8vo, 6s.

FIFTY YEARS; or, Dead Leaves and Living Seeds. By the Rev. HARRY JONES, Prebendary of St. Paul's; Author of "Holiday Papers," "East and West London," &c. Second Edition. Crown 8vo, 4s.

RECOLLECTIONS OF A MILITARY LIFE. By General Sir JOHN ADYE, G.C.B., R.A., late Governor of Gibraltar. With Illustrations by the Author. Demy 8vo, 14s. net.

THE REIGN OF QUEEN VICTORIA: A Survey of Fifty Years of Progress. Edited by T. HUMPHRY WARD. 2 vols. 8vo, 32s.

A COLLECTION OF LETTERS OF W. M. THACKERAY, 1847-1855. With Portraits and Reproductions of Letters and Drawings. Second Edition. Imperial 8vo, 12s. 6d.

HISTORY OF THE UNITED STATES. By E. BENJAMIN ANDREWS. D.D., LL.D., President of the Brown University. 2 vols. crown 8vo, with Maps, 16s.

IN STEVENSON'S SAMOA. By MARIE FRASER. Second Edition. With Frontispiece. Crown 8vo, 2s. 6d.

THE HAWARDEN HORACE. By CHARLES L. GRAVES, Author of "The Blarney Ballads," "The Green above the Red," &c. Third Edition. Small post 8vo, 3s. 6d.

THE MARTYRED FOOL. By D. CHRISTIE MURRAY, Author of "Rainbow Gold," "Aunt Rachel," "Joseph's Coat," &c. Crown 8vo, 6s.

A FATAL RESERVATION. By R. O. PROWSE, Author of "The Poison of Asps," &c. Crown 8vo, 6s.

GLEAMS OF MEMORY; with some Reflections. By JAMES PAYN. Second Edition. Crown 8vo, 3s. 6d.

THE WHITE COMPANY. By A. CONAN DOYLE, Author of "Micah Clarke," &c. Crown 8vo, 6s.

THE MASK AND THE MAN. By PERCY ANDREAE, Author of "Stanhope of Chester." Crown 8vo, 6s.

THE VAGABONDS. By MARGARET L. WOODS, Author of "A Village Tragedy," &c. Crown 8vo, limp red cloth, 2s. 6d.

GRANIA: the Story of an Island. By the Hon. EMILY LAWLESS. Crown 8vo, 3s. 6d.

ROBERT ELSMERE. By Mrs. HUMPHRY WARD, Author of "Marcella," "The History of David Grieve," &c. Popular Edition, crown 8vo, 6s.; CHEAP EDITION, crown 8vo, limp cloth, 2s. 6d.; Cabinet Edition, 2 vols. small 8vo, 12s.

By the same Author.

THE HISTORY OF DAVID GRIEVE. Popular Edition. Crown 8vo 6s. Cheap Edition. Crown 8vo, limp cloth, 2s. 6d.

MARCELLA. Popular Edition. Crown 8vo, 6s.

London: SMITH, ELDER, & CO., 15 Waterloo Place.

RENAISSANCE FANCIES
AND STUDIES

Printed by BALLANTYNE, HANSON & CO.
At the Ballantyne Press

TO

MY DEAR FRIENDS

MARIA AND PIER DESIDERIO PASOLINI

EASTER 1895

PREFACE

THESE essays being mainly the outcome of direct personal impressions of certain works of art and literature, and of the places in which they were produced, I have but few acknowledgments to make to the authors of books treating of the same subject. Among the exceptions to this rule, I must mention foremost Professor Tocco's *Eresia nel Medio Evo*, Monsieur Gebhart's *Italie Mystique*, and Monsieur Paul Sabatier's *St. François d'Assise*.

I am, on the other hand, very deeply indebted to the conversation and advice of certain among my friends, for furnishing me second-hand a little of that archæological and critical knowledge which is now-a-days quite unattainable save by highly trained specialists. My best thanks, therefore, to Miss Eugénie Sellers, editor of Furtwängler's "Masterpieces of Greek Sculpture;" to Mr. Bernhard Berenson, author of "Venetian Painters," and a monograph on Lorenzo

Lotto; and particularly to my friend Mrs. Mary Logan, whose learned catalogue of the Italian paintings at Hampton Court is sufficient warrant for the correctness of my art-historical statements, which she has had the kindness to revise.

MAIANO, NEAR FLORENCE,
April 1895.

CONTENTS

	PAGE
PREFACE .	ix
THE LOVE OF THE SAINTS .	1
THE IMAGINATIVE ART OF THE RENAISSANCE	65
TUSCAN SCULPTURE . . .	135
A SEEKER OF PAGAN PERFECTION, BEING THE LIFE OF DOMENICO NERONI, PICTOR SACRILEGUS	163
VALEDICTORY . . .	233

THE LOVE OF THE SAINTS

▲

I

"Panis Angelicus fit panis hominum. O res mirabilis, manducat Dominum Pauper, Servus et Humilis." These words of the Matins of the Most Holy Sacrament I heard for the first time many years ago, to the beautiful and inappropriate music of Cherubini. They struck me at that time as foolish, barbarous, and almost gross; but since then I have learned to think of them, and in a measure to feel of them, as of something greater and more solemn than all the music that Cherubini ever wrote.

All the hymns of the same date are, indeed, things to think upon. They affect one—the "Stabat Mater," for instance, and the "Ave Verum"—very much in the same way as the figures which stare down, dingy green and blue, from the gold of the Cosmati's mosaics: childish, dreary, all stiff and agape, but so solemn and pathetic, and full of the greatest future. For out of those Cosmati mosaics, and those barbarous frescoes of the old basilicas, will come Giotto and all the Renaissance; and out of those Church songs will come Dante; they are all signs, poor primitive rhymes and primitive figures, that the world is teeming again, and will bare, for centuries to come, new spiritual wonders. Hence the importance, the venerableness of all those mediæval hymns. But of none so much, to my mind, as of those words I have quoted from the Matins of the Most Holy Sacrament—

> "O res mirabilis, manducat Dominum,
> Pauper, Servus et Humilis."

For their crude and pathetic literality, their image of the Godhead actually giving Himself, as they emphatically say, to be *chewed* by the poor and humble man and the serf, show them to have been most especially born, abortions though they be, in the mightiest throes of mystical feeling, after the incubation of whole nations, born of the great mediæval marriage, sublime, grotesque, morbid, yet health-bringing, between abstract idealising religious thought and the earthly affections of lovers and parents—a strange marriage, like that of St. Francis and Poverty, of which the modern soul also had to be born anew.

Indeed, if we realise in the least what this hymn must have meant, shouted in the processions of Flagellants, chaunted in the Pacts of Peace after internecine town wars; above all, perhaps, muttered in the cell of the friar, in the den of the weaver; if we sum up, however inadequately, the state of things whence it arose, and whence it helped to deliver us, we may think that the greatest music is scarcely reverent enough to accompany these poor blundering rhymes.

The Feast of the Most Holy Sacrament, to whose liturgy this hymn, "O Res Mirabilis," belongs, was instituted to commemorate the miracle of Bolsena, which, coming late as it did, in the country of St. Francis, and within two years of the birth of Dante, seems in its significant coincidences, in its startling symbolism, the fit material summing up of what is conveniently designated as the Franciscan revival: the introduction into religious matters of passionate human emotion. For in the year 1263, at Bolsena in Umbria, the consecrated wafer dropped blood upon the hands of an unbelieving priest.

This trickery of a single individual, or more probably hallucination—this lie and self-delusion of interested or foolish bystanders—just happened to symbolise a very great reality. For during the earlier Middle Ages, before the coming of Francis of Assisi, the souls of men, or, more properly, their hearts, had been sorely troubled and jeopardised.

The mixture of races and civilisations, southern and northern and eastern, antique and barbarian, which had been slowly taking place ever since the fall of the Roman Empire, had seemed, in its consummation of the twelfth century, less fertile on the whole than poisonous. The old tribal system, the old civic system, triumphant centralising imperialism, had all been broken up long since; and now feudalism was going to pieces in its turn, leaving a chaos of filibustering princelets, among whom loomed the equivocal figures of Provençal counts, of Angevin and Swabian kings, brutal as men of the North, and lax as men of the South; moreover, suspiciously oriental; brilliant and cynical persons, eventually to be typified in Frederick II., who was judiciously suspected of being Antichrist in person. In the midst of this anarchy, over-rapid industrial development had moreover begotten the tendencies to promiscuity, to mystical communism, always expressive of deep popular misery. The Holy Land had become a freebooter's Eldorado; the defenders of Christ's sepulchre were turned half-Saracen, infected with unclean mixtures of creeds. Theology was divided between neo-Aristotelean logic, abstract and arid, and Alexandrian esoteric mysticism, quietistic, nay, nihilistic; and the Church had ceased to answer to any spiritual wants of the people. Meanwhile, on all sides everywhere, heresies were teeming, austere and equivocal, pure and unclean according to individuals, but all of them anarchical, and therefore destructive at a moment when, above all, order and discipline were wanted. The belief in the world's end, in the speedy coming of Antichrist and the Messiah, was rife among all sects; and learned men, the disciples of Joachim of Flora, were busy calculating the very year and month. Lombardy, and most probably the south of France, Flanders and the Rhine towns, were full of strange Manichean theosophies, pessimistic dualism of God and devil, in which God always got the worst of it, when God did not happen to be the devil himself. The ravening lions, the clawing, tearing griffins, the nightmare brood carved on the capitals, porches, and pulpits of pre-Franciscan churches, are surely not, as orthodox antiquarians assure us, mere fanciful symbols of the Church's vigilance and virtues: they express too well the far-spread occult Manichean spirit, the belief in a triumphant power of evil.

Michelet, I think, has remarked that there was a moment in the early Middle Ages when, in the mixture of all contrary things, in the very excess of spiritual movement, there seemed a possibility of dead level, of stagnation, of the peoples of Europe becoming perhaps bastard Saracens, as in Merovingian times they had become bastard Romans; a chance of Byzantinism in the West. Be this as it may, it seems certain that, towards the end of the twelfth century, men's souls were shaken, crumbling, and what was worse, excessively arid. There was as little certainty of salvation as in the heart of that Priest saying Mass at Bolsena; but the miracle came to mankind at large some seventy years before it came to him. It had begun, no doubt, unnoticed in scores of obscure heresies, in hundreds of unnoticed individuals; it became manifest to all the world in the persons of Dominick, of Elizabeth of Hungary, of King Lewis—above all, of Francis of Assisi. As in the hands of the doubting priest, so in the hands of all suffering mankind, the mystic wafer broke, proving itself true food for the soul: the life-blood of hope and love welled forth and fertilised the world. For the second time, and in far more humble and efficacious way, Christ had been given to man.

To absorb the Eternal Love, to feed on the Life of the World, to make oneself consubstantial therewith, these passionate joys of poor mediæval humanity are such as we should contemplate with sympathy only and respect, even when the miracle is conceived and felt in the grossest, least spiritual manner. That act of material assimilation, that feeding off the very Godhead in most literal manner, as described in the hymn to the Most Holy Sacrament, was symbolic of the return from exile of the long-persecuted instincts of mankind. It meant that, spiritually or grossly, each according to his nature, men had cast fear behind them, and—O res mirabilis! —grown proud once more to love.

Of this new wonder—questionable enough at times, but, on the whole, marvellously beneficent—the German knightly poets, so early in the field, are naturally among the earliest (for the Provençals belonged to a sceptical, sensual country) to give us a written record. Nearly all of the Minnesingers composed what we must call religious erotics, in no way different, save for names of Christ and the Virgin, from their most impassioned secular ones. The Song of Solomon, therefore, is one of the few pieces of written literature of which we find constant traces in the works of these very literally illiterate poets. Yet the quality of their love, if one may say so, is very different from anything Hebrew, or, for the matter of that, Greek or Roman; their ardour is not a transient phenomenon which disturbs them, like that of the Shulamite, or the lover described by Sappho or Plato, but a chief business of their life, as in the case of Dante, of Petrarch, of Francesca and Paolo, or Tristram and Yseult. Indeed, it is difficult to guess whether this self-satisfied, self-glorifying quality, which distinguishes mediæval passion from the passion (always regarded as an interlude, harmless or hurtful, in civic concerns) of unromantic Antiquity—whether, I say, this peculiarity of mediæval love is due to its having served for religious as well as for secular use, or whether the possibility of its being brought into connection with the highest mysteries and aspirations was not itself a result of the dignity in which mere earthly ardours had come to be held. Be this as it may, these German devotional rhapsodies display their essentially un-Hebrew, un-antique characters only the more by the traces of the *canticus canticorum* in them, as in all devout love lyrics.

Any one curious in such matters may turn to a very striking poem by Dante's contemporary, Frauenlob, in Von der Hagen's great collection. Also to a very strange composition, from the heyday of minne-song, by Heinrich von Meissen. This is not the furious love ode, but the ceremonious epithalamium of devotional poetry. It is the bearing in triumph, among flare of torches and incense smoke, over flower-strewn streets and beneath triumphal arches, of the Bride of the Soul, her enthroning on a stately couch, like some new-wed

Moorish woman, for men to come and covet and admire. Above all, and giving one a shock of surprise by association with the man's other work, is a very long and elaborate poem addressed to Christ or God by no less a minnesinger than Master Gottfried of Strasburg. In it the Beloved is compared to all the things desired by eye or ear or taste or smell: cool water and fruit slaking feverish thirst, lilies with vertiginous scent, wine firing the blood, music wakening tears, precious stones of Augsburger merchants, essences and spices of an Eastern cargo :—

> "Ach herzen Trut, genaden vol,
> Ach wol u je mer mere wol,
> Ein suez in Arzeniê
> Ach herzen bruch, ach herzen not.
> Ach Rose rot,
> Ach rose wandels vrie!
> Ach jugend in jugent, ach jugender Muot,
> Ach bluejender herzen Minne!"

And so on for pages; the sort of words which poor Brangwain may have overheard on the calm sea, when the terrible knowledge rushed cold to her heart that Tristram and Yseult had drained the fatal potion.

All this is foolish and unwholesome enough, just twice as much so, for its spiritual allegorising, as the worldly love poetry of these often foolish and unwholesome German chivalrous poets. But, for our consolation, in that same huge collection of Von der Hagen's Minnesingers, stand the following six lines, addressed to the Saviour, if tradition is correct, by a knightly monk, Bruder Wernher von der Tegernsee :—

> " Du bist mîn, ih bin dîn ;
> Des solt dû gewis sîn.
> Dû bist beslozzen
> In mînem herzen ;
> *Verlorn ist daz sluzzelîn :*
> *Dû muost immer drinne sîn.*"

"Thou art locked up in my heart; the little key is lost; thou must remain inside."

This is a way of loving not logically suitable, perhaps, to a divine essence, but it is the lovingness which fertilises the soul, and makes flowers bud and birds sing in the heart of man. Out of it, through simple creatures like Bruder Wernher, through the simplicity of scores of obscurer singers and craftsmen than he, of hundreds of nameless good men and women, comes one large half of the art of Dante and Giotto, nay, of Raphael and Shakespeare: the tenderness of the modern world, unknown to stoical Antiquity.

II

The early Middle Ages—the times before Love came, and with it the gradual dignifying of all realities which had been left so long to mere gross or cunning or violent men—the early Middle Ages have left behind them one of the most complete and wonderful of human documents, the letters of Abélard and Héloïse. This is a book which each of us should read, in order to learn, with terror and self-gratulation, how the aridity of the world's soul may neutralise the greatest individual powers for happiness and good. These letters are as chains which we should keep in our dwelling-place, to remind us of past servitude, perhaps to warn us against future.

No other two individuals could have been found to illustrate, by the force of contrast, the intellectual and moral aridity of that eleventh century, which yet, in a degree, was itself a beginning of better things. For Héloïse and Abélard were not merely among the finest intellects of the Middle Ages; they were both, in different ways, to the highest degree passionately innovating natures. No woman has ever been more rich and bold and warm of mind and heart than Héloïse; nor has any woman ever questioned the unquestioned ideas and institutions of her age, of any age, with such vehemence and certainty of intuition. She judges questions which are barely asked and judged of now-a-days, applying to consecrated sentimentality the long-lost instinctive human rationalism of the ancient philosophers. How could St. Luke recommend us to desist from getting back our stolen property? She feels, however obscurely, that this is foolish, antisocial, unnatural. Nay, why should God prefer the penitence of one sinner to the constant goodness of ninety-nine righteous men? She is, this learned theologian of the eleventh century, as passionately human in thought as any Mme. Roland or Mary Wolstonecraft of a hundred years ago.

Abélard, on the other hand, we know to have been one of the most subtle and solvent thinkers of the Middle Ages; pursued by the greatest theologians, crushed by two Councils, and remaining, in the popular fancy, as a sort of Friar Bacon, a forerunner of the wizard Faustus; a man whom Bernard of Clairvaux called a thief of souls, a rapacious wolf, a Herod; a man who reveals himself a Pagan in his attempts to turn Plato into a Christian; a man who disputes about Faith in the teeth of Faith, and criticises the Law in the name of the Law; a man, most enormous of all, who sees nothing as symbol or emblem (*per speculum et ænigmata*), but dares to look all things in the face (*facie ad faciem omnia intuetur*). *Facie ad faciem omnia intuetur*, this, which is the acknowledged method of all modern, as it had been of all antique, thought, nay, of all modern, all antique, all healthy spiritual life—this was the most damnable habit of Abélard; and, as the letters show, of Héloïse. What shall we think, in consequence, of the intellectual and moral sterility of the orthodox world of the eleventh century, when we find this heretical man, this rebellious woman, arguing incessantly about unrealities, crushing out all human feeling, judging all questions of cause and effect, settling all relations of life, with reference to a system of intricate symbolical riddles? These things are exceedingly difficult for a modern to realise; we feel as though we had penetrated into some Gulliver's world or kingdom of the Moon; for theology and its methods have been relegated, these many hundred years, to a sort of *Hortus inclusus* where nothing human grows. These mediæval men of science apply their scientific energies to mastering, collecting, comparing and generalising, not of any single fact of nature, but of the words of other theologians. The magnificent sense of intellectual duty, so evident in Abélard, and in a dozen monastic authors quoted by him, is applied solely to fantasticating over Scripture and its expositors, and diverting their every expression from its literal, honest, sane meaning. And indeed, are some of the high efforts of mediæval genius, the calculations of Joachim and the Eternal Gospel, any better than the Book of Dreams and the Key to the Lottery? Most odious, perhaps, in this theology triumphant (sickening enough, in good sooth, even in the timid official theology of later days), is the loss of all sense of what's what, of fitness and decency, which interprets allegorically the grosser portions of Scripture, and, by a reverse process, lends to the soul the vilest functions of the body, and discusses virtue in the terms of fleshliness. No knowledge can come out of this straw-splitting *in vacuo;* and certainly no art out of this indecent pedant's symbolism: all things are turned to dusty, dirty lumber.

As with the intellectual, so also, in large degree, with the moral: a splendid will to do right is applied, in its turn, to phantoms. Here again the letters of Abélard and Héloïse are extraordinarily instructive. The highest virtue, the all-including (how differently Dante feels, whatever he may say !), is *obedience*. Thus Abélard, having quoted from St. Augustine that all which is done for obedience' sake is well done, proceeds very logically : " It is more advantageous for us to act rightly than to do good. . . . We should think not so much of the action itself, as of the manner in which it is performed."

Do not imagine that this care for the motive and contempt of the action arises from an estimate of the importance of a man's sum-total of tendencies, contrasted with his single, perhaps unintentional, acts; still less that the advantage thus referred to has anything to do with other men's happiness. The advantage is merely to the individual soul, or in a cruder, truer view, to the individual combustible body to which that soul shall be eternally reunited hereafter. And the spirit which makes virtue alone virtuous is the spirit of obedience : obedience theoretically to a god, but practically to a father of the Church, a Council, an abbot or abbess. In this manner right-doing is emptied of all rational significance, becomes dependent upon what itself, having no human, practical reason, is mere arbitrary command. Chastity, for instance, which is, together with mansuetude, the especial Christian virtue, becomes in this fashion that mere guarding of virginity which, for some occult reason, is highly prized in Heaven ; as to clean living being indispensable for bearable human relations, which even the unascetic ancients recognised so clearly, there is never an inkling of that. Whence, indeed, such persons as do not *go in for* professionally pleasing the divinity, who are neither priests, monks, nor nuns, need not stickle about it; and the secular literature of the Middle Ages, with its Launcelots, Tristrams, Flamencas, and all its German and Provençal lyrists, becomes the glorification of illicit love. Indeed, in the letters before us, Abélard regrets his former misconduct only with reference to religious standards: as a layman he was perfectly free to seduce Héloïse; the scandal, the horrible sin, was not the seduction, but the profanation by married love of the dress of a nun, the sanctuary of the virgin. So it is with the renunciation of all the world's pleasures and interests. The ascetic sacrifice of inclination, which the stoics had conceived as resistance to the tyrant without and the tyrant within, as a method for serene and independent life and death, this ascetic renunciation becomes, in this arid theological world, the mere giving up to please a jealous God of all that is not He. Abélard's regulations for the nuns, which he gives as rules of perfection (save in the matter of that necessary half sin, marriage) to devout lay folk, come after all to this: give human nature enough to keep it going, so that it may be able to sacrifice everything else to the jealousy of the Godhead. Eating, clothing oneself, washing (though, by the way, there is no mention of this save for the sick), nay, speaking and thinking, are merely instrumental to the contemplation of God; any more than suffices for this is sinful. On this point

Abélard quotes, with stolidest approval, one of the most heart-rending of anecdotes. A certain monk being asked why he had fled humankind, answered, on account of his great love for it, and the impossibility of loving God and it at the same time.

Think upon that. Think on the wasted treasure of loving-kindness of which that monk and the thousands he represents cheated his fellow-men. O love of human creatures, of man for woman, parents and children, of brethren, love of friends; fuel and food, which keeps the soul alive, balm curing its wounds, or, if they be incurable, helps the poor dying thing to die at last in peace—this was those early saints' notion of thee!

To refuse thus to love is to refuse not merely the highest usefulness, but to refuse also the best kind of justice. Here again, nay, here more than ever, we may learn from those wonderful letters. They constitute, indeed, a document of the human soul to which, in my recollection, one other only, Benjamin Constant's *Adolphe*, can be compared. But in these letters,—hers of grief, humiliation, hopelessness, making her malign her noble self; and his, bitter, self-righteous, crammed with theological moralisings—we see not merely the dual drama of two ill-assorted creatures, but the much more terrible tragedy, superadded by the presence, looming, impassive, as of Cypris in Euripides' Hippolytus, of a third all-powerful and superhuman entity: the spirit of monasticism. The unequal misery, the

B

martyrdom of Héloïse arises herefrom, that she rebels against this *Deus ex machina;* that this nun of the eleventh century is a strong warm-hearted modern woman, fit for Browning. While Abélard is her whole life, the intimate companion of her highest thoughts, she is only a toy to him, and a toy which his theologian's pride, his monkish self-debasement, makes him afraid and ashamed of. Abélard has been for her, and ever remains, something like Brahma to Goethe's Bayadere; her love, her love above all for his intrepid intellect, has raised him to a sacredness so great, that his whim, his fame, his peace, his very petulance can be refused nothing; and that, on the other hand, any concession taken from him seems positive sacrilege. Hence her refusal of marriage, her answer, " that she would be prouder as his mistress—the Latin word is harlot—than as the wife of Cæsar." Fifty years later, in the kind, passionate, poetical days of St. Francis, Héloïse might have given this loving fervour to Christ, and been a happy, if a deluded, woman; but in those frigid monkish days, there was no one for her to love, save this frigid monkish Abélard. As it is, therefore, she loves Christ and God in obedience to Abélard; she passionately cons the fathers, the Scriptures, merely because, so to speak, the hand of Abélard has lain on the page, the eyes of Abélard have followed the characters; and finally, after all her vain entreaties for (she scarce knows what!) love, sympathy, one personal word, she feeds her starving heart on the only answer to her supplications—the dialectic exercises, metaphysical treatises, and theological sermons (containing even the forms applicable only to a congregation) which he doles out to her. Thankful for anything which comes *from* him, however little it comes *to* her.

How different with Abélard! Despite occasional atrocious misery and unparalleled temporal misfortunes (which on the whole act upon him as tonics), this great metaphysician is well suited to his times, and spiritually thrives in their exhausted, chill atmosphere. The public rumour (which Héloïse hurls at him in a fit of broken-hearted rage), that his passion for her had been but a passing folly of the flesh, he never denies, but, on the contrary, reiterates perpetually for her spiritual improvement; let her understand clearly from what inexpressible degradation God in His mercy has saved them, at least saved him; let her realise that he wanted only carnal indulgence, and would have got it, if need be, through threats and blows. He recognises, in his past, only a feeling which, now it is over, fills his ascetic mind with nothing but disgust and burning shame, and hence he tries, by degrading it still more, by cynically raking up all imaginable filth, to separate that past from his present. So far, were only he himself concerned, one would sympathise, though contemptuously, with this agonised reaction of a proud, perhaps a vain, *man* of mere intellect. But the atrocious thing is, that he treats her as a loathsome relic of this past dishonour; and answers her prayer (after twelve years' silence!) for a word of loving-kindness by elaborate denunciations of their former love, and reiterated jubilations that *he*, at least, has long been purged thereof; not unmixed with sharp admonishment that she had better not try to infect his soul afresh, but set about, if needful, cleansing her own. Now it so happens that what he would cure her of is incurable, being, in fact, eternal, divine—simple human love. So, to his pious and cynical admonitions she answers with strange inconsistency. Long brooding over his taunts will sometimes make her, to whom he is always the divinity, actually believe, despite her reiteration, that she had sinned out of obedience to him, that she really is a polluted creature, guilty of the unutterable crime of contaminating a man of God, nay, a god himself. And then, unable to silence affection, she cries out in agony at the perversity of her nature, incapable even of hating sincerely its sinfulness; for would she not do it again, is she not the same Héloïse who would have left the very altar, the very communion with Christ, at Abélard's word? At other times she is pious, resigned, almost serene; for is that not Abélard's wish? a careful mother to her nuns. But when, encouraged by her docility and blind to her undying love, Abélard believes that he has succeeded in quieting her down, and rewards her piety by some rhetorical phrase of Monkish eulogy, she suddenly turns round, a terrible tragic figure. She repudiates the supposed purity and piety, blazons out her wickedness and hypocrisy, and cries out, partly with the horror of the sacrilegious nun, mainly with the pride of the faithful wife, that it is not God she loves but Abélard.

After the most violent of these outbreaks there is a dead silence. One guesses that some terrible message has come, warning her that unless she promised that she would never write to Abélard save as the Abbess of the Paraclete to the monk of Cluny, not a word from him shall ever come; and that, in order to keep this last miserable comfort, she has bitten out that truth-speaking tongue of hers. For after this there are only questions on theological points and on the regulation of nunneries; and Abélard becomes as liberal of words as he used to be chary, as full of encouragement as he once was of insult, now that he feels comfortably certain that Héloïse has changed from a mistress to a penitent, and that in her also there is an end at last of all that sinful folly of love. And thus, upon Héloïse pacified, numbed, dead of soul, among her praying and scrubbing and cooking and linen-mending nuns; and Abélard reassured, serene, spiritually proud once more among the raging controversies, the ecclesiastical persecutions in which his soul prospered, the volume closes; the curtain falls upon one of the most terrible tragedies of the heart, as poignant after seven hundred years as in those early Middle Ages, before St. Francis claimed sun and swallows as brethren, and the baby Christ was given to hold to St. Anthony of Padua.

III

The humanising movement, due no doubt to greater liberty and prosperity, to the growing importance of honest burgher life, which the Church authorised in the person of Francis of Assisi, doubtless after persecuting it in the persons of dozens of obscure heresiarchs — this great revival of religious faith was essentially the triumph of profane feeling in the garb of religious: the sanctification, however much disguised, of all forms of human love. One is fully aware of the moral dangers attendant upon every such equivocation; and the great saints (like their last modern representatives, the fervent, shrewd, and kindly leaders of certain Protestant revivals) were probably, for all their personal extravagances, most fully prepared for every sort of unwholesome folly among their disciples. The whole of a certain kind of devotional literature, manuals of piety, Church hymns, lives and correspondence of saintly persons, is unanimous in testifying to the hysterical self-consciousness, intellectual enervation, emotional going-to-bits, and moral impotence produced by such vicarious and barren expenditure of feeling. Yet it seems to me certain that this enthroning of human love in matters spiritual was an enormous, indispensable improvement, which, whatever detriment it may have brought in individual and, so to say, professionally religious cases, nay, perhaps to all religion as a whole, became perfectly wholesome and incalculably beneficent in the enormous mass of right-minded laity.

For human emotion, although so often run to waste, had been at least elicited, and, once elicited, could find, in nine cases out of ten, its true and beneficent channel; whereas, in the earlier mediæval days, the effort to crush out all human feeling (as with that holy man quoted by Abélard), to break all human solidarity, had not merely left the world in the hands of unscrupulous and brutal persons, but had imprisoned all finer souls in solitary and selfish thoughts of their individual salvation. Things were now different. The story of Lucchesio of Poggibonsi, recovered from oblivion by M. Paul Sabatier, is the most lovely expression of Franciscan tenderness and reverence towards the affections of the laymen, and ought to be remembered in company with the legend of the wood-pigeons, whom St. Francis established in his cabin and blessed in their courtship and nesting. This Lucchesio had exercised a profession which has ever savoured of damnation to the minds of the poor and their lovers, that of corn merchant or speculator in grain; but touched by Franciscan preaching, he had kept only one small garden, which, together with his wife, he cultivated half for the benefit of the poor. One day the wife, known in the legend only as Bona Donna, sickened and knew she must die, and the sacrament was brought to her accordingly. But Lucchesio never thought that it could be God's will that he should remain on earth after his wife had been taken from him. So he got himself shriven, received the last sacraments with her, held her hands while she died ; and when she was dead, stretched himself out, made the sign of the cross, called on Jesus, Mary, and St. Francis, and peacefully died in his turn : God could not have wished him to live on without her. The passionate Franciscan sympathy with human love make light of all the accepted notions of bereavement being acceptable as a divine dispensation. Lucchesio of Poggibonsi was, we are told, a member of the Third Order of Franciscans, and his legend may help us to appreciate the value of such institutions, which gave heaven to the laity, to the married burgher, the artisan, the peasant; which fertilised the religious ideal with the simplest and sweetest instincts of mankind. But, Third Order apart, the mission of the regular Franciscans and Dominicans is wholly different from that of the earlier orders of monasticism proper. The earlier monks, however useful and venerable as tillers of the soil and students of all sciences, were, nevertheless, only agglomerated hermits, retired from the world for the safety each of his own soul; whereas the preaching, wandering friars are men who mix with the world for the sake of souls of others. Thus, throughout the evolution of religious communities, down to the Jesuits and Oratorians, to the great nursing brother- and sisterhoods of the seventeenth century, we can watch the substitution of care for lay souls in the place of more saintly ones—a gradual secularisation in unsuspected harmony with the heretical and philosophical movements which tend more and more to make religion an essential function of life, instead of an activity with which life is for ever at variance.

In accordance with this evolution is the great enthroning of love in the thirteenth century: it means the replacing of the terror of a divinity, who was little better than a metaphysical Moloch (sometimes, and oftener than we think, a metaphysical Ormuzd and Ahriman of Manichean character), by the idolatry of an all-gracious Virgin, of an all-compassionate and all-sympathising Christ.

It was an effort at self-righting of the unhappy world, this love-fever which followed on the many centuries of monastic self-mutilation; for, in sickness of the spirit, the hot stage, for all its delirium, means a possibility of life. Moreover, it gave to mankind a plenitude of happiness such as is necessary, whether reasonable or unreasonable, for mankind to continue living at all; art, poetry, freedom, all the things which form the *Viaticum* on mankind's journey through the dreary ages, requiring for their production, it would seem, an extra dose of faith, of hope, and happiness. Indeed, the Franciscan movement is important not so much for its humanitarian quality as for its optimism.

Many other religious movements have asserted, with equal and greater efficacy, the need for charity and loving-kindness; but none, as it seems to me, has conceived like it that charity and loving-kindness are not mitigations of misery, but aids to joy. The universal brotherhood, preached by Francis of Assisi, is a brotherhood not of suffering, but of happiness, nay, of life and of happiness.

The sun, in the wonderful song which he made—characteristically—during his sickness, is the brother of man because of his radiance and splendour; water and fire are his brethren on account of their virtues of purity and humbleness, of jocund and beautiful strength;[1] and if we find, throughout his legends, the Saint perpetually accompanied by birds—the swallows he begged to let him speak, the falcon who called him in the morning, the turtle-doves whose pairing he blessed, and all the feathered flock whom Benozzo represents him preaching to in the lovely fresco at Montefalco—if, as I say, there is throughout his life and thoughts a sort of perpetual

---

[1] St. Francis's hymn (Sabatier, *St. François d'Assise*):—

> Laudato sie, mi signore, cum tucte le tue creature,
> Spetialmento messer lo frate sole,
> Lo quale jorna, et illumini per lui;
> *Et ello è bello e radiante cum grande splendore.*
>
> . . . .
> Laudato si, mè signore per frate Vento
> Et per aere et nubilo et sereno et omne tempo
>
> . . . .
> Laudato, si, mi signore, per sor acqua
> La quale è multo utile et humele et pretiosa et casta;
> Laudato si, mi signore, per frate focu
> Per lo quale ennallumini la nocte
> *Et ello è bello et jocundo e robustioso e forte.*

In its rudeness, how magnificent is this last line!

whir and twitter of birds, it is, one feels sure, because the creatures of the air, free to come and go, to sit on beautiful trees, to drink of clear streams, to play in the sunshine and storm, able above all to be like himself, poets singing to God, are the symbols, in the eyes of Francis, of the greatest conceivable felicity.[1]

Indeed, we can judge of what the Franciscan movement was to the world by what its gospel, the divine *Fioretti*, are even to ourselves. This humble collection of stories and sayings, sometimes foolish, always childlike, becomes, to those who have read it with more than the eyes of the body, a beloved and necessary companion, like the solemn serene books of antique wisdom, the passionate bitter Book of Job, almost, in a way, like the Gospels of Christ. But not for the same reason: the book of Francis teaches neither heroism nor resignation, nor divine justice and mercy; it teaches love and joyfulness. It keeps us for ever in the company of creatures who are happy because they are loving: whether the creatures be poor, crazy Brother Juniper (the comic person of the cycle) eating his posset in brotherly hap-

---

[1] St. Francis's sermon to the birds in the valley of Bevagna (*Fioretti* xvi.): "Ancora gli (a Dio) siete tenuti per lo elemento dell' aria che egli ha diputato a voi . . . e Iddio vi pasce, e davvi li fiumi e le fonti per vostro bere; davvi li monti e le valli per vostro rifugio e gli alberi alti per fare li vostri nidi . . . e però guardatevi, sirocchie mie, del peccato della ingratitudine, e sempre vi studiate di lodare Iddio . . . e allora tutti qugli uccilli si levarons in aria con maraviglios canti."

Fioretti xxviii. " . . . Questo dono, che era dato a frate Bernardo da Quintevalle, cioè, che volando si pascesse come la rondine." *Fioretti* xxii., Considerazioni i.

piness with the superior he had angered; or Brother Masseo, unable from sheer joy in Christ to articulate anything save " U-u-u," "like a pigeon;" or King Lewis of France falling into the arms of Brother Egidio; or whether they be the Archangel Michael in friendly converse with Brother Peter, or the Madonna handing the divine child for Brother Conrad to kiss, or even the Wolf of Gubbio, converted, and faithfully fulfilling his bargain. There are sentences in the *Fioretti* such as exist perhaps in no other book in the world, and which teach something as important, after all, as wisdom even and perfect charity—"And there answered Brother Egidio: Beloved brethren, know that as soon as he and I embraced one another, the light of wisdom revealed and manifested to me his heart, and to him mine; and thus by divine operation, seeing one into the other's heart, that which I would have said to him and he to me, each understood much better than had we spoken with our tongue, and with greater joyfulness. . . ." Again, Jesus appeared to Brother Ruffino and said, "Well didst thou do, my son, inasmuch as thou believedst the words of St. Francis; for he who saddened thee was the demon, whereas I am Christ thy teacher; and for token thereof I will give thee this sign: As long as thou live, thou shalt never feel affliction of any sort nor sadness of heart."

St. Francis, we are told, being infirm of body, was comforted through God's goodness by a vision of the joy of the blessed. "Suddenly there appeared to him an angel in a great radiance, which angel held a viol in his left hand and a bow in his right. And while St. Francis remained in stupefaction at the sight, this angel drew the bow once *upwards* across the viol, and instantly there issued such sweetness of melody as melted the soul of St. Francis, and suspended it from all bodily sense. And, as he afterwards told his companions, he was of opinion that if that angel had drawn the bow *downwards* (instead of upwards) across the viol, his soul would have departed from his body for the very excess of delight."

It was not so much to save the souls of men from hell, about which, indeed, there is comparatively little talk in the *Fioretti*, but to draw them also into the mystic circle where such angelic music was heard, that Francis of Assisi preached throughout Umbria, and even as far as the Soldan's country; and, if we interpret it rightly, the strings of that heavenly viol were the works of creation and the souls of all creatures, and the bow, whose upward movement ravished, and whose downward movement would have almost annihilated with its sweetness, that bow drawn across the vibrating world was no other than love.

IV

Justice preached by Hebrew prophets, charity and purity taught by Jesus of Nazareth, fortitude recommended by Epictetus and Aurelius, none of these great messages to men necessarily produce that special response which we call Art. But the message of loving joyfulness, of happiness in the world and the world's creatures, whether men or birds, or sun or moon,—this message, which was that of St. Francis, sets the soul singing; and just such singing of the soul makes art. Hence, even as the Apennine blazed with supernatural light, and its forests and rocks became visible to the most distant wayfarers, when the Eternal Love smote with its beams the praying saint on La Vernia; so also the souls of those men of the Middle Ages were made luminous and visible by the miracle of poetry and painting, and we can see them still, distinct even at this distance.

One of the earliest of the souls so revealed is that of the Blessed Jacopone of Todi. Jacopo dei Benedetti, a fellow-countryman of St. Francis, must have been born in the middle of the thirteenth century, and is said to have died in 1316, when Dante, presumably, was writing his "Purgatory" and "Paradise;" to him is ascribed the authorship of the hymn "Stabat Mater," remembered, and to be remembered (owing to the embalming power of music) far beyond his vernacular poems. Tradition has it that he turned to the religious life in consequence of the sudden death of his beloved, and the discovery that she had worn a hair-shirt next her delicate body. Be this as it may, many allusions in his poems suggest that he had lived the wild life of the barbarous Umbrian cities, being a highwayman perhaps, forfeiting his life, and also having to fly the country before the fury of some family vendetta. On the other hand, it is plain at every line that he was a frantic ascetic, taking a savage pleasure in vilifying all mundane things, and passionately disdainful of study, of philosophical and theological subtleties. No poet, therefore, of the troubadour sort, or of the idealising learned refinement of Guinicelli or Cavalcanti. Nor was his life one of apostolic sweetness. Having taken part in the furious Franciscan schism, and pursued with invectives Boniface VIII., he was cast by that Pope into a dungeon at Palestrina. "My dwelling," he writes, "is subterranean, and a cesspool opens on to it; hence a smell not of musk. No one can speak to me; the man who waits on me may, but he is obliged to make confession of my sayings. I wear jesses like a falcon, and ring whenever I move: he who comes near my room may hear a queer kind of dance. When I have laid myself down, I am tripped up by the irons, and wound round in a big chain (*negli ferri inzampagliato, inguainato in catenone*). I have a little basket hung up so that the mice may not injure it; it can hold five loaves. . . . While I eat them little by little, I suffer great cold."

Moreover, Pope Boniface refuses him absolution, and Jacopone's invectives are alternated with heart-rending petitions that this mercy at least be shown him; as to his other woes, he will endure them till his death. In this frightful place Jacopone had visions, which the Church, giving him therefore the title of Blessed, ratifies as genuine. One might expect nightmares, such as troubled the early saints in the wilderness, or John Bunyan in gaol; but that was not the spirit of the mediæval revival: terror had been cast out by love. More than a quarter of Jacopone's huge volume consists in what is merely love poetry: he is languishing, consumed by love; when the beloved departs, he sighs and weeps, and shrieks, and *dies alive.* Will the beloved have no mercy? "Jesu, donami la morte, o di te fammi assaggiare." Then the joys of love, depicted with equal liveliness, amplifications as usual of the erotic hyperboles of the Shulamite and her lover; the phenomenon, to whose uncouth strangeness devotional poetry accustoms us even now-a-days, which we remarked in Gottfried von Strasburg and Frauenlob, and on which it is needless further to insist.

But there is here in Jacopone something which we missed in Gottfried and Frauenlob, of which there is no trace in the Song of Solomon, but which, suggested in the lovely six lines of Bruder Wernher, makes the emotionalism of the Italian Middle Ages wholesome and fruitful. A child-like boy and girlish light-heartedness that makes love a matter not merely of sighing and dying, but of singing and dancing; and, proceeding thence, a fervour of loving delightedness which is no longer of the man towards the woman, but of the man and the woman towards the baby. The pious monk, in his ecstasies over Jesus, intones a song which might be that of those passionate *farandoles* of angels who dance and carol in Botticelli's most rapturous pictures:—

> "Amore, amor, dove m'hai tu menato?
> Amore, amor, fuor di me m'hai trattato.
> Ciascun amante, amator del Signore,
> Venga alla danza cantando d'amore."

Can we not see them, the souls of such fervent lovers, swaying and eddying, with joined hands and flapping wings, flowers dropping from their hair, above the thatched roof of the stable at Bethlehem?

The stable at Bethlehem! It is perpetually returning to Jacopone's thoughts. The cell, the dreadful underground prison at Palestrina, is broken through, irradiated by visions which seem paintings by Lippo or Ghirlandaio, nay, by Correggio and Titian themselves, "the tender baby body (*il tenerin corpo*) of the blood of Mary has been given in charge to a pure company; St. Joseph and the Virgin contemplate the little creature (*il piccolino*) with stupefaction. *O gran piccolino Jesu nostro diletto*, he who had seen Thee between the ox and the little ass, breathing upon thy holy breast, would not have guessed thou were begotten of the Trinity!" But besides the ox and the ass there are the angels. " In the worthy stable of the sweet baby the angels are singing round the little one; they sing and cry out, the beloved angels, quite reverent, timid and shy (*tutti riverenti, timidi e subbietti*, this beautiful expression is almost impossible save in Italian), round the little baby Prince of the Elect who lies naked among the prickly hay. He lies naked and without covering; the angels shout in the heights. And they wonder greatly that to such lowliness the Divine Verb should have stooped. The Divine Verb, which is highest knowledge, this day seems as if He knew nothing of anything (*il verbo divino che è sommo sapiente, in questo di par che non sappia niente!*). Look at him on the hay, crying and kicking (*che gambetta piangente*), as if He were not at all a divine man....." Meanwhile, other angels, as in Benozzo's frescoes, are busy "picking rarest flowers in the garden." In the garden! Why He Himself is a fragrant garden; Jesus is a garden of many sweet odours; and "what they are those can tell who are the lovers of this sweet little brother of ours."

Di Questo nostro dolce fratellino: it is such expressions as these, Bambolino, Piccolino, Garzolino, "el magno Jesulino," these caressing, ever-varied diminutives, which make us understand the monk's passionate pleasure in the child; and which, by the emotion they testify to and re-awaken, draw more into relief, make visible and tangible the little kicking limbs on the straw, the dimpled baby's body.

And then there are the choruses of angels. "O new song," writes Jacopone, " which has killed the weeping of sick mankind! Its melody, methinks, begins upon the high *Fa*, descending gently on the *Fa* below, which the *Verb* sounds. The singers, jubilating, forming the choir, are the holy angels, singing songs in that hostelry, before the little babe, who is the Incarnate Word. On lamb's parchment, behold! the divine note is written, and God is the scribe, Who has opened His hand, and has taught the song."

Have we not here, in this odd earliest allegory of music and theology, this earliest precursor of the organ-playing of Abt Vogler, one of those choirs, clusters of singing childish heads—clusters, you might almost say, of sweet treble notes, tied like nosegays by the score held scrollwise across them, which are among the sweetest inventions of Italian art, from Luca della Robbia to Raphael, "cantatori, guibilatori, che tengon il coro?"

And this is the place for a remark which, in the present uncertainty of all æsthetic psychology, I put forward as a mere suggestion, but a suggestion less wide of the truth than certain theories now almost unquestioned: the theories which arbitrarily assume that art is the immediate and exact expression of contemporary spiritual aspirations and troubles. That such may be the case with literature, particularly the more ephemeral kinds thereof, is very likely, since literature, save in the great complex structures of epos, tragedy, choral lyric, is but the development of daily speech, and possibly as upstart, as purely passing, as daily speech itself; moreover, in its less artistic forms, requiring little science or apprenticeship.

But art is a thing of older ancestry; you cannot, however bursting with emotion, embody your feelings in forms like those of Phidias, of Michelangelo, of Bach, or Mozart, unless such forms have come ready to hand through the long, steady working of generations of men: Phidias and Bach in person, cut off from their precursors, would not, for all their genius, get as far as a schoolboy's caricature, or a savage's performance on a marrow-bone. And these slowly elaborated forms, representing the steady impact of so many powerful minds, representing, moreover, the organic necessity by which, a given movement once started, that movement is bound to proceed in a given direction, these forms cannot be altered, save infinitesimally, to represent the particular state of the human soul at a given moment. You might as well suppose that the human shape itself, evolved through these millions of years, could suddenly be accommodated to perfect representation of the momentary condition of certain human beings; even the Tricoteuses of the guillotine had the heads and arms of ordinary women, not the beaks and claws of harpies. Hence such expressiveness must be limited to microscopic alterations; and, indeed, one marvels at the modest demands of the art critics, who are satisfied with the pucker of a frontal muscle of a Praxitelean head as testimony to the terrible deep disorder in the post-Periclean Greek spirit, and who can still find in the later paintings of Titian, when all that makes Titian visible and admirable is deducted, a something, just a little *je ne sais quoi*, which proves these later Titians to have originated in the Catholic reaction. If the theory of art as the outcome of momentary conditions be limited to such particularities, I am quite willing to accept it; only, such particularities do not constitute the large, important and really valuable characteristics of art, and it matters very little by what they are produced.

How then do matters stand between art and civilisation? Here follows my hypothesis. There is in the history of every art (and for brevity's sake, I include in this term every distinct category, say, renaissance sculpture as distinguished from antique, of the same art) a moment when, for one reason or other, that art begins to come to the fore, to bestir itself. The circumstances of the nation and time make this art materially advantageous or spiritually attractive; the opening up of quarries, the discovery of metallic alloys, the necessity of roofing larger spaces, the demand for a sedentary amusement, for music to dance to in new social gatherings—any such humble reason, besides many others, can cause one art to issue more particularly out of the limbo of the undeveloped, or out of the lumber-room of the unused.

It is during this historic moment—a moment which may last years or scores of years—that, as it seems to me, an art can really be deeply affected by its surrounding civilisation. For is it not called forth by that civilisation's requirements, material or spiritual; and is it not, by the very fact of being thus new, or at all events nascent, devoid of all conditioning factors, save those which the civilisation and its requirements impose from without? An art, like everything vital, takes shape not merely by pressure from without, but much more by the necessities inherent in its own constitution, the almost mechanical necessities by which all variable things *can* vary only in certain fashions. All the natural selection, all the outer pressure in the world, cannot make a stone become larger by cutting, cannot make colour less complex by mixing, cannot make the ear perceive a dissonance more easily than a consonance, cannot make the human mind turn back from problems once opened up, or revert instantaneously to effects it is sick of; and a number of such immutable necessities constitute what we call the organism of an art, which can therefore respond only in one way and not another to the influences of surrounding civilisation. Given the sculpture of the Ægina period, it is impossible we should not arrive at the sculpture of the time of Alexander: the very constitution of clay and bronze, of marble, chisel and mallet, let alone that of the human mind, makes it inevitable; and you would have it inevitably if you could invert history, and put Chæronea in the place of Salamis. But there is no reason why you should eventually get Lysippian and Praxitelean sculpture instead of Egyptian or Assyrian, say, in the time of Homer, whenever that may have been. For the causes which forced Greek sculpture along the line leading to Praxiteles and Lysippus were not yet at work; and had other forces, say, a preference for stone work instead of clay and bronze work, a habit of Persian or Gaulish garments, of Lydian effeminate life instead of Dorian athleticism, supervened, had satraps ordered rock-reliefs of battles instead of burghers ordering brazen images of boxers and runners, Praxiteles and Lysippus might have remained *in mente Dei*, if, indeed, even there. Similarly, once given your Pisan sculptors, Giotto, nay, your imaginary Cimabue, you inevitably get your Donatello, Masaccio, Ghirlandajo, and eventually your Leonardo, Michelangelo, and Titian; for the problems of form and of sentiment, the questions of perspective, anatomy, dramatic expression, lyric suggestion, architectural decoration, were established, in however rudimentary a manner, as soon as painting was ordered to leave off doing idle, emotionless Christs, rows of gala saints and symbols of metaphysic theology, and told to set about showing the episodes of Scripture, the things Christ and the Apostles did, and the places where they did them, and the feelings they felt about it all; told to make visible to the eye the gallant archangels, the lovable Madonnas, the dear little baby Saviours, the angels with their flowers and songs, all the human hope and pity and passion and tenderness which possessed the world in the days of St. Francis.

What pictures should we have seen if Christianity (which was impossible) had continued in the habits of thought and feeling of the earlier Middle Ages? Byzantine *icones* become frightfuler and frightfuler, their theological piety perhaps sometimes relieved by odd wicked Manichean symbolism; all talent and sentiment abandoning painting, perhaps to the advantage of music, whose solemn period of recondite contrapuntal complexity—something corresponding to the ingenuities and mysticism of theology—might have come two centuries earlier, and delighted the world instead of being unnoticed by it. Be this as it may, there is no need for wondering, as people occasionally wonder, how the solemn terror, the sweetness, pathos, or serenity of men like Signorelli, Botticelli, or Perugino, nay Michelangelo, Raphael, or Giorgione, could have originated among Malatestas, Borgias, Poggios, or Aretines. It did not. And, therefore, since literature always precedes its more heavily cumbered fellow-servant art, we must look for the literary counterpart of the painters of the Renaissance among the writers who preceded them by many generations, men more obviously in touch with the great mediæval revival: Dante, Boccaccio, the compilers of the "Fioretti di San Francesco," and, as we have just seen, Fra Jacopone da Todi.

V

What art would there have been without that Franciscan revival, or rather what emotional synthesis of life would art have had to record? This speculation has been dismissed as futile, because it is impossible to conceive that mankind could have gone on without some such enthusiastic return of faith in the goodness of things. But another question remains to be answered, remains to be asked; and that is, what was the spiritual meaning of the art which immediately preceded the Franciscan revival? what was the emotional synthesis of life given by those who had come too early to partake in the new religion of love?

The question seems scarcely to have occurred to any one, perhaps because the Church found it expedient to obliterate, to the best of her power, all records of her terrible mediæval vicissitudes, and to misinterpret, for the benefit of purblind antiquarians, the architectural symbolism of the earlier Middle Ages.

Since, in the deciphering of such expressions of mankind's moods and intuitions, scientific investigation is scarcely more important than the moods and intuitions of the looker-on, it seems quite fitting that I should begin these suggestions about pre-Franciscan Italian art by saying that some years ago there met by accident in my mind a certain impression of Lombard twelfth-century art, and a certain anecdote of Lombard twelfth-century history.

It was at Lucca, a place most singularly rich in round-arched buildings, that I was, so to speak, overwhelmed by the fact that the Italian churches of immediately pre-Franciscan days possess by way of architectural ornamentation nothing but images of deformity and emblems of wickedness. This fact, apart from its historical bearing, may serve also to illustrate a theory I have already put forth, to wit, that the only art which is necessarily expressive of contemporary thought and feeling is such as embodies very little skill, and as expresses but very few organic necessities of form, both of which can result only from the activity and the influence of generations of craftsmen; since in these Lucchese churches the architectural forms proclaim one thing and the sculptural details another. The first speak only of logic and serenity; the second only of the most abominable nightmare. The truth is, that these churches of Lucca, and their more complex and perfect prototypes, like Sant' Ambrogio of Milan, and San Miniato of Florence, are not the real outcome of the century which built them. It is quite natural that, with their stately proportions, their harmonious restrained vaultings, their easy, efficient colonnades, their ample and equable illumination, above all their obvious pleasure in constructive logic, these churches should affect us as being *classic* as opposed to romantic, and even in a very large measure actually antique; for they have come, through generations as long-lived and as scanty as those of the patriarchs, straight from the classic, the antique; grandchildren of the courts of law and temples of Pagan Rome, children of the Byzantine basilicas of early Christian days; strange survivals from distant antiquity, testifying to the lack of artistic initiative in the barbarous centuries between Constantine to Bar-

barossa. No period in the world's history could have produced anything so organic without the work of previous periods; and when the Middle Ages did in their turn produce an architecture original to themselves, it was by altering these still classic forms into something absolutely different: that thirteenth-century Gothic which answers to the material and necessities of the democratic and romantic times heralded by St. Francis. The twelfth century, therefore, could not express itself in the architectural forms and harmonies of those Lucchese churches; but it could express itself in their rude and thoroughly original sculpture. Hence, while there is in them no indication of the symbolism of the coming ogival Gothic, there is no trace either of the symbolism belonging to Byzantine buildings. None of the Gothic imagery testifying faith and joy in God and His creatures; no effigies of saints; at most only of the particular building's patron; no Madonnas, infant Christs, burning cherubim, singing and playing angels, armed romantic St. Michael or St. George; none of those goodly rows of kings and queens guarding the portals, or of those charming youthful heads marking the spring of the pointed arch, the curve of the spandril. Nor, on the other hand, any remnant of Byzantine devices of the date-loaded palms, the peacocks and doves, the bunches of grapes, the serene, almost Pagan imagery which graces the churches of the Cœlian and Aventine, the basilicas of Ravenna, and which would seem the necessary accompaniment of this stately

Neo-Byzantine architecture. The churches of Lucca, like their contemporaries and immediate predecessors throughout Tuscany and North Italy, are ornamented only with symbols of terror.[1]

The minds of the sculptors seem haunted by the terror of wicked wild beasts, irresistible and mysterious, as in the night fears of children. The chief ornament of St. Michael of Lucca is a curious band of black and white inlaid work, of which Mr. Ruskin has said, with the optimism of an orthodox symbolist, that it shows that the people of Lucca loved hunting, even as the people of Florence loved the sciences and crafts symbolised on their belfry. But the two or three solitary mannikins of the frieze of St. Michael exemplify not the pleasures, but the terrors of the chase; or rather they are not hunting, but being hunted by the wild beasts all round; attacked rather than pursuing, flying on their little horses from the unequal fight, or struggling under the hug of bears, the grip of lions; never

[1] The Cathedral of Assisi, a very early mediæval building, affords a singular instance of the meeting of the last remnant of that serene symbolism of Roman and Byzantine-Roman churches with the usual Lombard horrors. A fine passion-flower or vine encircles the porch, peacocks strut and drink from an altar, while, on the other hand, lions mangle a man and a sheep, and horrible composite monsters, resembling the prehistoric plesiosaurus, bite each other's necks. A Madonna and Christ are enthroned on Byzantine seats, the weight resting on human beings, not so realistically crushed as those of Ferrara and Milan, but suffering. There is a similar meeting of symbols in the neighbouring Cathedral of Foligno; and, so far as I could see, the Umbrian valley is rich in very early churches of this type, sometimes lovely in ornamentation, like S. Pietro of Spoleto, sometimes very rude, like the tiny twin churches of Bevagna.

does one of them carry off a dead creature or deal a mortal blow. The wild beasts are masters of the situation, the men mere intruders, speedily worsted; and this is proved by the fact that where the wolves, lions, and bears are not struggling with human beings, they are devouring each another, the appearance of the poor little scared men being only an interlude in the everlasting massacre of one beast by another. The people who worked this frieze may have pretended, perhaps, that they were expressing the pleasures of hunting; but what they actually realised was evidently the horrors of a world given over to ravening creatures. The porch sculptures of this and all the other churches of Lucca remove all further doubt upon this point. For here what human beings there lie under the belly and in the claws (sometimes a mere horrid mangled human head) of the lions and lionesses who project like beamheads out of the wall or carry the porch columns on their back: scowling, murderous creatures, with which the twelfth and early thirteenth century ornamented even houses and public tanks like Fonte Branda, which less terrified generations adorned with personified virtues. The nightmare of wild beasts is carried on in the inside of the churches: there again, under the columns of the pulpits are the lions and lionesses gnashing their teeth, tearing stags and gazelles and playing with human heads. And, to increase the horror, there also loom on the capitals of the nave strange unknown birds of prey, fantastic terrible vultures and griffins.

Everywhere massacre and nightmare in those churches of Lucca. And the impression they made on my mind was naturally strengthened by the recollection of the similar and often more terrible carvings in other places, Milan, Pavia, Modena, Volterra, the Pistoiese and Lucchese hill-towns, in all other places rich in pre-Franciscan art. Above all, there came to my mind the image of the human figures which in most of such pre-Franciscan places express the other half of all this terror, the feelings of mankind in this kingdom of wicked, mysterious wild beasts. I allude to the terrible figures, crushed into dwarfs and hunchbacks by the weight of porch columns and pulpits, amid which the tragic creature, with broken spine and starting eyes, of Sant' Ambrogio of Milan is, through sheer horrified realisation, a sort of masterpiece. But there are wild beasts, lions and lionesses, among the works of thirteenth-century sculptors, and lions and lionesses continue for a long time as ornaments of pure Gothic architecture. Of course; but it was the very nearness of the resemblance of these later creatures that brought home to me the utterly different, the uniform and extraordinary character, of those of earlier date: the emblem was kept by the force of tradition, but the meaning thereof was utterly changed. The Pisani, for instance, carved lions and lionesses under all their pulpits; some of them are merely looking dignified, others devouring their prey, but they are conceived by a semi-heraldic decorator or an intelligent naturalist; nay, the spirit of St. Francis has entered into the sculptors, the feeling for animal piety and happiness, to the extent of representing the lionesses as suckling and tenderly licking their whelps. The men of that time cannot even conceive, in their newly acquired faith and joy in God and His creatures, what feelings must have been uppermost in the men who first set the fashion of adorning churches with men-devouring monsters.

Such were my impressions during those days spent among the serene Lucchese churches and their terrible emblems. And under their influence, thinking of the times which had built the churches and carved the emblems, there came to my memory a very curious anecdote, unearthed by the learned ecclesiastical historian Tocco, and consigned in his extremely suggestive book on mediæval heresies. A certain priest of Milan became so revered for his sanctity and learning, and for the marvellous cures he worked, that the people insisted on burying him before the high altar, and resorting to his tomb as to that of a saint. The holy man became even more undoubtedly saintly after his death; and in the face of the miracles which were wrought by his intercession, it became necessary to proceed to his beatification. The Church was about to establish his miraculous sainthood, when, in the official process of collecting the necessary information, it was discovered that the supposed saint was a Manichean heretic, a *Catharus*, a believer in the wicked Demiurgus, the creating Satan, the defeat of the spiritual God, and the uselessness of the coming of Christ. It was quite probable that he had spat upon the crucifix as a symbol of the devil's triumph; it was quite possible that he had said masses to Satan as the true creator of all matter. Be this as it may, that priest's half-canonised bones were publicly burnt and their ashes scattered to the wind. The anecdote shows that the Manichean heresies, some ascetic and tender, others brutal and foul, had made their way into the most holy places. And, indeed, when we come to think of it, no longer startled by so extraordinary a revelation, this was the second time that Christianity ran the risk of becoming a dualistic religion—a religion, like some of its Asiatic rivals, of pessimism, transcendentally spiritual or cynically base according to the individual believer. Nor is it surprising that such views, identical with those of the transcendental theologians of the fourth century, and equivalent to the philosophical pessimism of our own day, as expounded particularly by Schopenhauer, should have found favour among the best and most thoughtful men of the early Middle Ages. In those stern and ferocious, yet tender-hearted and most questioning times, there must have been something logically satisfying, and satisfying also to the harrowed sympathies, in the conviction, if not in the dogma, that the soul of man had not been made by the maker of the foul and cruel world of matter; and that the suffering of all good men's hearts corresponded with the suffering, the humiliation of a mysteriously dethroned God of the Spirit. And what a light it must have shed, completely solving all terrible questions, upon the story of Christ's martyrdom, so constantly uppermost in the thoughts and feelings of mediæval men!

Now, the men who built Sant' Ambrogio[1] and San Miniato a Monte, who carved the stone nightmares, the ravening lions, the squashed and writhing human figures of the early Lombard and Tuscan churches, were the contemporaries of that Manichean priest of Milan, who, although a saint, had believed in the triumph of the Devil and the wickedness of the Creator. And among his fellow-heretics—those heretics lurking everywhere, and most among the most religious—should we not expect to find the mysterious guilds of Lombard freemasons, and the craftsmen to whom they gradually revealed their secrets, affirming in their stone symbolism to the already initiated, and suggesting to the uninitiated, their terrible creed of inevitable misery on earth? Nay, can we not imagine some of them, even as the Templars were accused of doing (and the Templars were patrons, remember, of important guilds of masons),

---

[1] Here are a few dates, as given by Murray's Handbooks.
Fiesole Cathedral begun 1028; S. Miniato a Monte, 1013; Pisa Cathedral consecrated 1118; baptistery (lower storey), 1153. Lucca façade (interior later), 1204; S. Frediano of Lucca begun by Perharit 671, altered in twelfth century; S. Michele façade, 1188. Pistoia: S. Giovanni Evangelista by Gruamons, 1166; S. Andrea, also by Gruamons; S. Bartolomeo by Rudolphinus, 1167. Pulpit of S. Ambrogio of Milan, 1201; church traditionally begun about 868, probably much more modern.

propitiating the Great Enemy by service and ritual, proclaiming his Power, even as the ancients propitiated the divinities of darkness whom they hated ? For the God of Good, we can fancy them reasoning, the Pure Spirit who will triumph when all this cruel universe goes to pieces, can wish for no material altars, and can have no use for churches. Or did not the idea of a dualism become confused into a vacillating, contradictory notion of a Power at once good and evil, something inscrutable, unthinkable, but inspiring less confidence than terror?

Whatever the secret of those sculptured monsters, this much is historically certain, that a dualistic, profoundly pessimist belief had honeycombed Christianity throughout Provence and Northern and Central Italy. But for this knowledge it would be impossible to explain the triumphant reception given to St. Francis and his sublime, illogical optimism, his train of converted wolves, sympathising birds, and saints and angels mixing familiarly with mortal men. The Franciscan revival has the strength and success of a reaction. And in sweeping away the pessimistic terrors of mankind, it swept away, by what is at least a strange coincidence, the nightmare sculpture of the old Lombard stonemasons.

What the things were which made room for the carved virgins and saints, the lute-playing angels and nibbling squirrels and twittering birds of Gothic sculpture, I wish to put before the reader in one significant example. The Cathedral of Ferrara is a building which, although finished in the thirteenth century, had been begun and consecrated so early as 1135, and the porch thereof, as is frequently the case, appears to have been erected earlier than other portions. Of this porch two pillars are supported by life-sized figures, one bearded, one beardless, both dressed in the girdled smock of the early Middle Ages. The enormous weight of the porch is resting, not conventionally (as in the antique caryatid) on the head, but on the spine; and the head is protruded forwards in a fearful effort to save itself, the face most frightfully convulsed: another moment and the spine must be broken and the head droop freely down. Before the portals, but not supporting anything, are six animals of red marble—a griffin, two lions, two lionesses, or what seem such, and a second griffin. The central lions are well preserved, highly realistic, but also decorative; one of them is crushing a large ram, another an ox, both creatures splendidly rendered. I imagine these central lions to be more recent (having perhaps replaced others) than their neighbours, which are obliterated to the extent of being lions or lionesses only by guesswork. These nameless feline creatures hold what appear to be portions of sheep, one of them having at its flank a curious excrescence like the stinging scorpion of the Mithra groups. The griffins, on the other hand, although every detail is rubbed out, are splendid in power and expression—great lion-bodied creatures, with gigantic eagle's beak, manifestly birds rather than beasts, with the muscular neck and probably the movement of a hawk. Like hawks, they have not swooped on to their prey, but let themselves drop on to it, arriving not on their belly like lions, but on their wings like birds. The prey is about a fourth of the griffin's size. One of the griffins has swooped down upon a wain, whose two wheels just protrude on either side of him; the heads of two oxen are under his paws, and the head, open mouthed, with terrified streaming hair, of the driver; beasts and men have come down flat on their knees. The other griffin has captured a horse and his rider; the horse has shied and fallen sideways beneath the griffin's loins, with head protruding on one side and hoofs on the other, the empty stirrup is still swinging. The rider, in mail-shirt and Crusader's helmet, has been thrown forward, and lies between the griffin's claws, his useless triangular shield clasped tight against his breast. Perhaps merely because the attitude of the two griffins had to be symmetrical, and the horse and rider filled up the space under their belly less closely than the cart, oxen, and driver, there arises the suggestive fact that the poor man and his bullocks are crushed more mercilessly than the rich man and his horse. But be this as it may, poor and rich, serf and knight, the griffin of destiny encompasses and pounces upon each; and the talons of evil pin down and the beak of misery rends with impartial cruel certainty.

Such is the account of the world and man, of justice and mercy, recorded for us by the stonemasons of Ferrara.

VI

As with the emotional, the lyric element in Renaissance art, so also with the narrative or dramatic; it belongs not to the original, real, or at all events primitive Christianity of the time when the Man Jesus walked on earth in the body, but to that day when He arose once more, no less a Christ, be sure, in the soul of those men of the Middle Ages. The Evangelists had never felt—why should they, good, fervent Jewish laymen?—the magic of the baby Christ as it was felt by those mediæval ascetics, suddenly reawakened to human feeling. There is neither tenderness nor reverence in the Gospels for the mother of the Lord; some rather rough words on her motherhood; and that mention in St. John, intended so evidently to bring the Evangelist, or supposed Evangelist, into closer communion with Christ, not to draw attention to Christ's mother. Yet out of those slight, and perhaps almost contemptuous indications, the Middle Ages have made three or four perfect and wonderful types of glorified womanhood: the Mother in adoration, the crowned, enthroned Virgin, the Mater Gloriosa; the broken-hearted Mother, Mater Dolorosa, as found at the foot of the cross or fainting at the deposition therefrom; types more complete and more immortal than that of any Greek divinity; above all, perhaps, the mere young mother holding the child for kindly, reverent folk to look at, for the little St. John to play with, or alone, looking at it, thinking of it in solitude and silence: the whole lovingness of all creatures rising in a clear flame to heaven. Nay, is not the suffering Christ a fresh creation of the Middle Ages, made really to bear the sorrows of a world more sorrowful than that of Judea? That strange Christ of the Resurrection, as painted occasionally by Angelico, by Pier della Francesca, particularly in a wonderful small panel by Botticelli; the Christ not yet triumphant at Easter, but risen waist-high in the sepulchre, sometimes languidly seated on its rim, stark, bloodless, with scarce seeing eyes, and the motionless agony of one recovering from a swoon, enduring the worst of all his martyrdom, the return to life in that chill, bleak landscape, where the sparse trees bend in the dawn wind; returning from death to a new, an endless series of sufferings, even as that legend made him answer the wayfaring Peter, *returning to be crucified once more—iterum crucifigi.*

All this is the lyric side, on which, in art as in poetry, there are as many variations as there are individual temperaments, and the variety in Renaissance art is therefore endless. Let us consider the narrative or dramatic side, on which, as I have elsewhere tried to show, all that could be done was done, only repetition ensuing, very early in the history of Italian art, by the Pisans, Giotto and Giotto's followers.

These have their counterpart, their precursors, in the writers and reciters of devotional romances.

Among the most remarkable of these is the "Life of the Magdalen," printed in certain editions of Frate Domenico Cavalca's well known charming translations of St. Jerome's "Lives of the Saints." Who the author may be seems quite doubtful, though the familiar and popular style might suggest some small burgher turned Franciscan late in life. As the spiritual love lyrics of Jacopone stand to the *Canzonieri* of Dante and of Dante's circle of poets, so does this devout novel stand to Boccaccio's more serious tales, and even to his "*Fiammetta*;" only, I think that the relation of the two novelists is the reverse of that of the poets; for, with an infinitely ruder style, the biographer of the Magdalen, whoever he was, has also an infinitely finer psychological sense than Boccaccio. Indeed, this little novel ought to be reprinted, like "Aucasin et Nicolette," as one of the absolutely satisfactory works, so few but so exquisite, of the Middle Ages.

It is the story of the relations of Jesus with the family of Lazarus, whose sister Mary is here identified with the Magdalen; and it is, save for the account of the Passion, which forms the nucleus, a perfect tissue of inventions. Indeed, the author explains very simply that he is narrating not how he knows of a certainty that things did happen, but how it pleases him to think that they might have happened. For the man puts his whole heart in the story, and alters, amplifies, explains away till his heart is satisfied. The Magdalen, for instance, was not all the sort of woman that foolish people think. If she took to scandalous courses, it was only from despair at being forsaken by her bridegroom, who left her on the wedding-day to follow Christ to the desert, and who was no other than the Evangelist John. Moreover, let no vile imputations be put upon it; in those days, when everybody was so good and modest, it took very little indeed (in fact, nothing which our wicked times would notice at all) to get a woman into disrepute.

Judged by our low fourteenth-century standard, this sinning Magdalen would have been only a little over-cheerful, a little free, barely what in the fourteenth century is called (the mere notion would have horrified the house of Lazarus) *a trifle fast;* our unknown Franciscan—for I take him to be a Franciscan—insists very much on her having sung and whistled on the staircase, a thing no modest lady of Bethany would then have done; but which, my dear brethren, is after all . . . .

This sinful Magdalen, repenting of her sins, such as they are, is living with her sister Mary and her brother Lazarus; the whole little family bound to Jesus by the miracle which had brought Lazarus back to life. Jesus and his mother are their guests during Passion week; and the awful tragedy of the world and of heaven passes, in the anonymous narrative, across the narrow stage of that little burgher's house. As in the art of the fifteenth century, the chief emotional interest of the Passion is thrown not on the Apostles, scarcely on Jesus, but upon the two female figures, facing each other as in some fresco of Perugino, the Magdalen and the Mother of Christ. Facing one another, but how different! This Magdalen has the terrific gesture of despair of one of those colossal women of Signorelli's, flung down, as a town by earthquake, at the foot of the cross. She was pardoned " because she had loved much ", —*quia multo amavit.* The unknown friar knew what *that* meant as well as his contemporary Dante, when Love showed him the vision of Beatrice's death. Never was there such heart-breaking as that of his heroine: she becomes almost the chief personage of the Passion; for she knows not merely all the martyrdom of the Beloved, feels all the agonies of His flesh and His spirit, but knows—how well!—that she has lost Him. Opposite this terrible convulsive Magdalen, sobbing, tearing her hair and rolling on the ground, is the other heart-broken woman, the mother; but how different! She remains maternal through her grief, with motherly thoughtfulness for others; for to the real mother (how different in this to the lover!) there will always remain in the world some one to think of. She bridles her sorrow; when John at last hesitatingly suggests that they must not stay all night on Calvary, she turns quietly homeward; and, once at home, tries to make the mourners eat, tries to eat with them, makes them take rest that dreadful night. For such a mother there shall not be mere bitterness in death; and here follows a most beautiful and touching invention: the glorified Christ, returning from Limbo, takes the happy, delivered souls to visit his mother.

"And Messer Giesù having tarried awhile with them in that place, said: 'Now let us go and make my mother happy, who with most gentle tears is calling upon me.' And they went forthwith, and came to the room where our Lady was praying, and with gentle tears asking God to give her back her son, saying it was to-day the third day. And as she stayed thus, Messer Giesù drew near to her on one side, and said: 'Peace and cheerfulness be with thee, Holy Mother.' And straightway she recognised the voice of her blessed son, and opened her eyes and beheld him thus glorious, and threw herself down wholly on the ground and worshipped him. And the Lord Jesus knelt himself down like her; and then they rose to their feet and embraced one another most sweetly, and gave each other peace, and then went and sat together," while all the holy people from Limbo looked on in admiration, and knelt down one by one, first the Baptist, and Adam and Eve, and all the others, saluting the mother of Christ, while the angels sang the end of all sorrows.

VII

There would be much to say on this subject. One might point out, for instance, not only that Dante has made the lady he loved in his youth into the heroine— a heroine smiling in fashion more womanlike than theological—of his vision of hell and heaven; but what would have been even less possible at any previous moment of the world's history, he has interwoven his theogony so closely with strands of most human emotion and passion (think of that most poignant of love dramas in the very thick of hell!), that, instead of a representation, a chart, so to speak, of long-forgotten philosophical systems, his poem has become a picture, pattern within pattern, of the life of all things: flowers blowing, trees waving, men and women moving and speaking in densest crowds among the flaming rocks of hell, the steps of purgatory, the planispheres of heaven's stars making the groundwork of that wondrous tapestry. But it is better to read Dante than to read about Dante, so I let him be.

On the other hand, and lest some one take Puritanic umbrage at my remarks on early Italian art, and deprecate the notion that religious painters could be so very human, I shall say a few parting words about the religious painter, the saint *par excellence*, I mean the Blessed Angelico. Heaven forbid I should attempt to turn him into a brother Lippo, of the Landor or Browning pattern! He was very far indeed, let alone from profanity, even from such flesh and blood feeling as that of Jacopone and scores of other blessed ones. He was, emotionally, rather bloodless; and whatsoever energy he had probably went in tussels with the technical problems of the day, of which he knew much more, for all his cloistered look, than I suspected when I wrote of him before. Angelico, to return to the question, was not a St. Francis, a Fra Jacopone. But even Angelico had his passionately human side, though it was only the humanness of a nice child. In a life of hard study, and perhaps hard penance, that childish blessed one nourished childish desires—desires for green grass and flowers, for gay clothes,[1] for prettily-dressed pink and lilac playfellows, for the kissing and hugging in which he had no share, for the games of the children outside the convent gate. How human, how ineffably full of a good child's longing, is not his vision of Paradise! The gaily-dressed angels are leading the little cowled monks—little baby black and white things, with pink faces like sugar lambs and Easter rabbits—into deep, deep grass quite full of flowers, the sort of grass every child on this wicked earth has been cruelly forbidden to wade in! They fall into those angels' arms, hugging them with the fervour of children in the act of *loving* a cat or a dog. They join hands with those angels, outside the radiant pink and blue toy-box towers of the celestial Jerusalem, and go singing "Round the Mulberry Bush" much more like the babies in Kate Greenaway's books than like the Fathers of the Church in Dante. The joys of Paradise, for this dear man of God, are not confined to sitting *ad dexteram domini*. . . .

Di questo nostro dolce Fratellino; that line of Jacopone da Todi, hymning to the child Christ, sums up, in

[1] Mme. Darmesteter's charming essays "The End of the Middle Ages," contain some amusing instances of such repressed love of finery on the part of saints. Compare Fioretti xx., "And these garments of such fair cloth, which we wear (in Heaven) are given us by God in exchange for our rough frocks."

the main, the vivifying spirit of early Italian art; nay, is it not this mingled emotion of tenderness, of reverence, and deepest brotherhood which made St. Francis claim sun and birds, even the naughty wolf, for brethren? This feeling becomes embodied, above all, in the very various army of charming angels; and more particularly, perhaps, because Venice had no other means of expression than painting, in the singing and playing angels of the old Venetians. These angels, whether they be the girlish, long-haired creatures, robed in orange and green, of Carpaccio; or the naked babies, with dimpled little legs and arms, and filetted silky curls of Gian Bellini, seem to concentrate into music all the many things which that strong pious Venice, tongue-tied by dialect, had no other way of saying; and we feel to this day that it sounds in our hearts and attunes them to worship or love or gentle contemplation. The sound of those lutes and pipes, of those childish voices, heard and felt by the other holy persons in those pictures—Roman knight Sebastian, Cardinal Jerome, wandering palmer Roch, and all the various lovely princesses with towers and palm boughs in their hands—moreover brings them together, unites them in one solemn blissfulness round the enthroned Madonna. These are not people come together by accident to part again accidentally; they are eternal, part of a vision disclosed to the pious spectator, a crowning of the Mass with its wax-lights and songs.

But the Venetian playing and singing angels are there for something more important still. Those excellent old painters understood quite well that in the midst of all this official, doge-like ceremony, it was hard, very hard lines for the poor little Christ Child, having to stand or lie for ever, for ever among those grown-up saints, on the knees of that majestic throning Madonna; since the oligarchy, until very late, allowed no little playfellow to approach the Christ Child, bringing lambs and birds and such-like, and leading Him off to pick flowers as in the pictures of those democratic Tuscans and Umbrians. None of that silly familiarity, said stately Venetian piety. But the painters were kinder. They incarnated their sympathy in the baby music-making angels, and bade them be friendly to the Christ Child. They are so; and nowhere does it strike one so much as in that fine picture, formerly called Bellini, but more probably Alvise Vivarini, at the Redentore, where the Virgin, in her lacquer-scarlet mantle, has ceased to be human altogether, and become a lovely female Buddha in contemplation, absolutely indifferent to the poor little sleeping Christ. The little angels have been sorry. Coming to make their official music, they have brought each his share of heaven's dessert: a little offering of two peaches, three figs, and three cherries on one stalk (so precious therefore !), placed neatly, spread out to look much, not without consciousness of the greatness of the sacrifice. They have not, those two little angels, forgotten, I am sure, the gift they have brought, during that rather weary music-making before the inattentive Madonna. They keep on thinking how Christ will awake to find all those precious things, and they steel their little hearts to the sacrifice. The little bird who has come (invited for like reason) and perched on the curtain bar, understands it all, respects their feelings, and refrains from pecking.

Such is the heart of the saints, and out of it comes the painted triumph of *El Magno Jesulino*.

angels, I myself, I am sure, that till they have been it,
dainty that nother we up und fes thing is bu t the
badeville' Bid mar. They keep on thinking how
Christ will aware to find all. To o pro bas tha t a,
and they read their Bible books in the sacristy. The
It is told who has come (twelve) for like reason, and
p what en t o certain long und a nd it all, expects
choir. They entertain from getting

Just it's a image of the Lady, and out of it comes
the Church of N. W. de Aparecida.

THE IMAGINATIVE ART OF THE
RENAISSANCE

E

I

In a Florentine street through which I pass most days, is a house standing a little back (the place is called the Square of Purgatory), the sight of which lends to that sordid street of stained palace backs, stables, and dingy little shops, a certain charm and significance, in virtue solely of three roses carved on a shield over a door. The house is a humble one of the sixteenth century, and its three roses have just sufficient resemblance to roses, with their pincushion heads and straight little leaves, for us to know them as such. Yet that rude piece of heraldic carving, that mere indication that some one connected with the house once thought of roses, is sufficient, as I say, to give a certain pleasurableness to the otherwise quite unpleasurable street.

This is by no means an isolated instance. In various places, as emblems of various guilds or confraternities, one meets similarly carved, on lintel or escutcheon, sheaves of lilies, or what is pleasanter still, that favourite device of the Renaissance (become well known as the monogram of the painter Benvenuto Garofalo), a jar with five clove-pinks. And on each occasion of meeting them, that carved lily and those graven clove-pinks, like the three roses in the Square of Purgatory, have shed a charm over the street, given me a pleasure more subtle than that derived from any bed of real lilies, or pot of real clove-pinks, or bush of real roses; colouring and scenting the street with this imaginary colour and perfume. What train of thought has been set up? It would be hard to say. Something too vague to be perceived except as a whole impression of pleasure; a half-seen vision, doubtless, of the real flowers, of the places where they grow; perhaps even a faint reminiscence, a dust of broken and pounded fragments, of stories and songs into which roses enter, or lilies, or clove-pinks.

Hereby hangs a whole question of æsthetics. Those three stone roses are the type of one sort of imaginative art; of one sort of art which, beyond or independent of the charm of visible beauty, possesses a charm that acts directly upon the imagination. Such charm, or at least such interest, may be defined as the literary element in art; and I should give it that name, did it not suggest a dependence upon the written word which I by no means intend to imply. It is the element which, unlike actual representation, is possessed by literature as well as by art; indeed, it is the essence of the former, as actual representation is of the latter. But it belongs to art, in the cases when it belongs to it at all, not because the artist is in any way influenced by the writer, but merely because the forms represented by the artist are most often the forms of really existing things, and fraught, therefore, with associations to all such as know them; and because, also, the artist who presents these forms is a human being, and as such not only sees and draws, but feels and thinks; because, in short, literature being merely the expression of habits of thought and emotion, all such art as deals with the images of real objects tends more or less, in so far as it is a human being, to conform to its type.

This is one kind of artistic imagination, this which I have rudely symbolised in the symbol of the three carved roses—the imagination which delights the mind by holding before it some charming or uncommon object, and conjuring up therewith a whole train of feeling and fancy; the school, we might call it, of intellectual decoration, of arabesques formed not of lines and colours, but of associations and suggestions. And to this school of the three carved roses in the Square of Purgatory belong, among others, Angelico, Benozzo, Botticelli, and all those Venetians who painted piping shepherds, and ruralising magnificent ladies absorbed in day-dreams.

But besides this kind of imagination in art, there is another and totally different. It is the imagination of how an event would have looked; the power of understanding and showing how an action would have taken place, and how that action would have affected the bystanders; a sort of second-sight, occasionally rising to the point of revealing, not merely the material aspect of things and people, but the emotional value of the event in the eyes of the painter. Thus, for instance, Tintoret concentrated a beam of sunlight into the figure of Christ before Pilate, not because he supposed Christ to have stood in that sunlight, but because the white figure, shining yet ghost-like, seemed to him, perhaps unconsciously, to indicate the position of the betrayed Saviour among the indifference and wickedness of the world. Hence I would divide all imaginative art, particularly that of the old Italian masters, into art which stirs our own associations, and suggests to us trains of thought and feeling perhaps unknown to the artist, and art which exhibits a scene or event foreign to ourselves, and placed before us with a deliberate intention. Both are categories of imaginative activity due to inborn peculiarities of character; but one of them, namely, the suggestive, is probably spontaneous, and quite unintentional, hence never asked for by the public, nor sought after by the artist; while the other, self-conscious and intentional, is therefore constantly sought after by the artist, and bargained for by the public. I shall begin with the latter, because it is the recognised commodity: artistic imagination, as bought and sold in the market, whether of good quality or bad.

II

The painters of the late thirteenth and early fourteenth century, developing the meagre suggestions of Byzantine decoration, incorporating the richer inventions of the bas-reliefs of the Pisan sculptors and of the medallions surrounding the earliest painted effigies of holy personages, produced a complete set of pictorial themes illustrative of Gospel history and of the lives of the principal saints. These illustrative themes—definite conceptions of situations and definite arrangements of figures—became forthwith the whole art's stock, universal and traditional; few variations were made from year to year and from master to master, and those variations resolved themselves continually back into the original type. And thus on, through the changes in artistic means and artistic ends, until the Italian schools disappeared finally before the schools of France and Flanders. Let us take a striking example. The presentation of the Virgin remains unaltered in main sentiment and significance of composition, despite the two centuries and more which separate the Gaddi from Titian and Tintoret, despite the complete change in artistic aims and methods separating still more completely the men of the fourteenth century from the men of the sixteenth. The long flight of steps stretching across the fresco in Santa Croce stretches also across the canvas of the great Venetians; and the little girl climbs up them alike, presenting her profile to the spectator; although at the top of the steps there is in one case a Gothic portal, and in the other a Palladian portico, and at the bottom of the steps in the fresco stand Florentines who might personally have known Dante, and at the bottom of the steps in the pictures the Venetian patrons of Aretino. Yet the presentation of the little maiden to the High Priest is quite equally conceivable in many other ways and from many other points of view. As regards both dramatic conception and pictorial composition, the moment might have been differently chosen; the child might still be with its parents or already with the priest; and the flight of steps might have been replaced by the court of the temple. Any man might have invented his own representation of the occurrence. But the men of the sixteenth century adhered scrupulously or indifferently to the inventions of the men of the fourteenth.

This is merely one instance in a hundred. If we summon up in our mind as many as we can of the various frescoes and pictures representing the chief incidents of Scripture history, we shall find that, while there are endless differences between them with respect to drawing, anatomy, perspective, light and shade, colour and handling, there are but few and slight variations as regards the conception of the situation and the arrangement for the figures. In the Marriage of the Virgin the suitors are dressed, sometimes in the loose robe and cap with lappets of the days of Giotto, and sometimes in the tight hose and laced doublet of the days of Raphael and of Luini; but they break their wands across their knees with the same gesture and expression; and although the temple is sometimes close at hand, and sometimes a little way off, the wedding ceremony invariably takes place outside it, and not inside. The shepherds in the Nativity are sometimes young and sometimes old, but they always come in broad daylight, and the manger by which the Virgin is kneeling is always outside the stable, and always in one corner of the picture. Again, whatever slight difference there may be in the expression and gesture of the apostles at the Last Supper, they are always seated on one side only of a table facing the spectator, with Judas alone on a stool on the opposite side. And although there are two themes of the Entombment of Christ, one where the body is stretched on the ground, the other where it is being carried to the sepulchre, the action is always out of doors, and never, as might sometimes be expected, gives us the actual burial in the vault. These examples are more than sufficient. Yet I feel that any description in words is inadequate to convey the extreme monotony of all these representations, because the monotony is not merely one of sentiment by selection of the dramatic moment, but of the visible composition of the paintings, of the outlines of the groups and the balancing of them. A monotony so complete that any one of us almost knows what to expect, in all save technical matters and the choice of models, on being told that in such a place there is an old Italian fresco, or panel, or canvas, representing some principal episode of Gospel history.

The explanation of this fidelity to one theme of representation in an art which was the very furthest removed from any hieratic prescriptions, in an art which was perpetually growing—and growing more human and secular—must be sought for, I think, in no peculiarities of spiritual condition or national imagination, but in two facts concerning the merely technical development of painting, and the results thereof. These two facts are briefly: that at a given moment—namely, the end of the thirteenth century and the beginning of the fourteenth—there existed just enough power of imitating nature to admit of the simple indication of a dramatic situation, without further realisation of detail; and that at this moment, consequently, there originated such pictorial indications of the chief dramatic situations as concerned the Christian world. And secondly, that from then and until well into the sixteenth century, the whole attention of artists was engrossed in changing the powers of indication into powers of absolute representation, developing completely the drawing, anatomy, perspective, colour, light and shade, and handling, which Giotto and his contemporaries had possessed only in a most rudimentary condition, and which had sufficed for the creation of just such pictorial themes as they had invented, and no more.

Let me explain myself further. The artists of the

fourteenth century, with the exception of Giotto himself—to whose premature excellence none of his contemporaries and disciples ever attained—give us, by means of pictorial representation, just about the same as could be given to us by the conventional symbolism of writing. In describing a Giottesque fresco, or panel, we are not stopped by the difficulty of rendering visible effects in words, because the visible effects that meet us are in reality so many words; so that, to describe the picture, it almost suffices to narrate the story, no arrangements of different planes and of light and shade, no peculiarities of form, foreshortening, colour, or texture requiring to be seen in order to be fully understood. The artists of the fifteenth century—for the Giottesques do little more than carry, without developing them, the themes of Giotto into various parts of Italy—work at adding to the art exactly those qualities which belong exclusively to it, and which baffle the mere written word: they acquire the means, slowly and laboriously, of showing these events no longer merely to the mind, but also to the eye; they place these people in real space, in real relations of distance and light, they give them a real body which can stand and move, made of real flesh and blood and bones, and covered with real clothes; they turn these abstractions once more into realities like the realities of nature whence they had been abstracted. But the work of the fifteenth century does not go beyond filling up the programme indicated by the

Giottesques; and it is only after the men of the sixteenth century have been enabled to completely realise all that the men of the fourteenth century had indicated, that art, with Michelangelo, Tintoret, and still more with the great painters of Spain and Flanders, proceeds to encounter problems of foreshortening, of light and shade, of atmospheric effect, that could never have been imagined by the contemporaries of Giotto, nor even by the contemporaries of Ghirlandaio and the Bellini. Hence, throughout the fifteenth century, while there is a steady development of the artistic means required to realise those narrative themes which the Giottesques had invented, there is no introduction of any new artistic means unnecessary for this result, but which, like the foreshortenings of Michelangelo, and the light and shade of Tintoret, like the still further additions to painting represented by men like Velasquez and Rembrandt, could suggest new treatment of the old histories and enable the well-known events to be shown from totally new intellectual standpoints, and in totally new artistic arrangements. If we look into the matter, we shall recognise that the monotony of representation throughout the Renaissance can be amply accounted for without referring to the fact, which, however, doubtless went for something, that the men of the fifteenth century were too much absorbed in the working out of details to feel any desire for new pictorial versions of the stories of the Gospel, and the lives of the Saints.

Moreover, the Giottesques—among whom I include the immediate precursors, sculptors as well as painters, of Giotto—put into their Scripture stories an amount of logic, of sentiment, of dramatic and psychological observation and imagination more than sufficient to furnish out the works of three generations of later comers. Setting aside Giotto himself, who concentrates and diffuses the vast bulk of dramatic invention as well as of artistic observation and skill, there is in even the small and smallest among his followers, an extraordinary happiness of individual invention of detail. I may quote a few instances at random. It would be difficult to find a humbler piece of work than the so-called Tree of the Cross, in the Florentine Academy: a thing like a huge fern, with medallion histories in each frond, it can scarcely be considered a work of art, and stands halfway between a picture and a genealogical tree. Yet in some of its medallions there is a great vivacity of imaginative rendering; for instance, the Massacre of the Innocents represented by a single soldier, mailed and hooded, standing before Herod on a floor strewn with children's bodies, and holding up an infant by the arm, like a dead hare, preparing slowly to spit it on his sword; and the kiss of Judas, the soldiers crowding behind, while the traitor kisses Christ, seems to bind him hand and foot with his embraces, to give him up, with that stealthy look backwards to the impatient rabble—a representation of the scene, infinitely superior in its miserable execution to Angelico's Ave Rabbi! with its elaborate landscape of towers and fruit trees. Again, in a series of predella histories of the Virgin, in the same place, also a very mediocre and anonymous work, there is extraordinary charm in the conception of the respective positions of Mary and Joseph at their wedding: he is quite old and grey; she young, unformed, almost a child, and she has to stand on two steps to be on his level, raising her head with a beautiful, childlike earnestness, quite unlike the conventional bridal timidity of other painters. Leaving these unknown mediocrities, I would refer to the dramatic value (besides the great pictorial beauty) of an Entombment by Giottino, in the corridor of the Uffizi: the Virgin does not faint, or has recovered (thus no longer diverting the attention from the dead Saviour to herself, as elsewhere), and surrounds the head of her son with her arms; the rest of the figures restrain themselves before her, and wink with strange blinking efforts to keep back their tears. Still more would I speak of two small frescoes in the Baroncelli Chapel at Santa Croce, which are as admirable in poetical conception as they are unfortunately poor in artistic execution. One of them represents the Annunciation to the Shepherds: they are lying in a grey, hilly country, wrapped in grey mists, their flock below asleep, but the dog vigilant, sniffing the supernatural. One is hard asleep; the other awakes suddenly, and has turned over and looks up screwing his eyes at the angel, who comes in a pale yellow winter sunrise cloud, in the cold, grey mist veined with yellow. The chilliness of the mist at dawn, the wonder of the vision, are felt with infinite charm. In the other fresco the three kings are in a rocky place, and to them appears, not the angel, but the little child Christ, half-swaddled, swimming in orange clouds on a deep blue sky. The eldest king is standing, and points to the vision with surprise and awe; the middle-aged one shields his eyes coolly to see; while the youngest, a delicate lad, has already fallen on his knees, and is praying with both hands crossed on his breast. For dramatic, poetic invention, these frescoes can be surpassed, poor as is their execution, only by Giotto's St. John ascending slowly from the open grave, floating upwards, with outstretched arms and illumined face, to where a cloud of prophets, with Christ at their head, enwraps him in the deep blue sky.

These pictorial themes elaborated by the painters of the school of Giotto were not merely as good, in a way, as any pictorial themes could be: simple, straightforward, often very grand, so that the immediately following generations could only spoil, but not improve upon them; they were also, if we consider the matter, the only pictorial representations of Scripture histories possible until art had acquired those new powers of foreshortening, and light and shade and perspective, which were sought for only after the complete attainment of the more elementary powers which the Giottesques never fully possessed. Let us ask ourselves how, in the fourteenth or fifteenth centuries, any notable change in general arrangement of any well-known Scripture subject could well have been introduced; and, in order to do so, let us realise one or two cases where the same subjects have been treated by later masters. Tintoretto's Last Judgment, where the Heavenly Hosts brood, poised on their wings, above the river of hell which hurries the damned down its cataracts, is impossible so long as perspective and foreshortening will barely admit (as is the case up to the end of the fifteenth century), of figures standing firmly on the ground and being separated into groups at various distances. In Rembrandt's and Terburg's Adoration of the Shepherds, the light emanates from the infant Christ; in Ribera's magnificent Deposition from the Cross, the dead Saviour and His companions are represented, not, as in the Entombments of Perugino and Raphael, in the open air, but in the ghastly light of the mouth of the sepulchre. These are new variations upon the hackneyed themes, but how were they possible so long as the problems of light and shade were limited (as was the case even with Leonardo), to giving the modelling, rather in form than in colour, of a face or a limb? One of the earliest and greatest innovations is Signorelli's treatment of the Resurrection in the chapel of San Brizio, at Orvieto; he broke entirely with the tradition (exemplified particularly by Angelico) of making the dead come fully fleshed and dressed as in their lifetime from under the slabs of a burial place, goaded by grotesque devils with the snouts and horns of weasels and rams, with the cardboard masks of those carnival mummers who gave the great pageant of Hell mentioned by old chroniclers. But Signorelli's innovation, his naked figures partially fleshed and struggling through the earth's crust, his naked demons shooting through the air and tying up the damned, could not possibly have been executed or even conceived until his marvellous mastery of the nude and of the anatomy of movement had been obtained. Indeed, wherever, in the art of the fifteenth century, we find a beginning of innovation in the conception and arrangement of a Scripture history, we shall find also the beginning of the new technical method which has suggested such a partial innovation. Thus, in the case of one of the greatest, but least appreciated, masters of the early Renaissance, Paolo Uccello. His Deluge, in the frescoes of the green cloister of S. Maria Novella, is wonderfully original as a whole conception; and the figure clinging to the side of the ark, with soaked and wind-blown drapery; the man in a tub trying to sustain himself with his hands, the effort and strain of the people in the water, are admirable as absolute realisation of the scene. Again, in the Sacrifice of Noah, there is in the foreshortened figure of God, floating, brooding, like a cloud, with face downward and outstretched hands over the altar, something which is a prophecy, and more than a prophecy, of

F

what art will come to in the Sixtine and the Loggie.
But these inventions are due to Uccello's special and
extraordinary studies of the problems of modelling and
foreshortening; and when his contemporaries try to
assimilate his achievements, and unite them with the
achievements of other men in other special technical
directions, there is an end of all individual poetical
conception, and a relapse into the traditional arrangements; as may be seen by comparing the Bible stories
of Paolo Uccello with those of Benozzo Gozzoli at Pisa.
It is not wonderful that the painters of the fifteenth
century should have been satisfied with repeating the
themes left by the Giottesques. For the Giottesques
had left them, besides this positive heritage, a negative
heritage, a programme to fill up, of which it is difficult
to realise the magnitude. The work of the Giottesques
is so merely poetic, or at most so merely decorative in
the sense of a mosaic or a tapestry, and it is in the
case of Giotto and one or two of his greatest contemporaries, particularly the Sienese, so well-balanced
and satisfying as a result of its elementary nature
that we are apt to overlook the fact that everything
in the way of realisation as opposed to indication,
everything distinguishing the painting of a story from
the mere telling thereof, remained to be done. And
such realisation could be attained only through a
series of laborious failures. It is by comparing some
of the later Giottesques themselves, notably the Gaddi
with Giotto, that we bring home to ourselves, for

instance, that Giotto did not, at least in his finest work at Florence, attempt to model his frescoes in colour. Now the excessive ugliness of the Gaddi frescoes at St. Croce is largely due to the effort to make form and boss depend, as in nature, upon colour. Giotto, in the neighbouring Peruzzi and Bardi chapels, is quite satisfied with outlining the face and draperies in dark paint, and laying on the colour, in itself beautiful, as a child will lay it on to a print or outline drawing, filling up the lines, but not creating them. I give this as a solitary instance of one of the first and most important steps towards pictorial realisation which the great imaginative theme-inventors left to their successors. As a fact, the items at which the fifteenth century had to work are too many to enumerate; in many cases each man or group of men took up one particular item, as perspective, modelling, anatomy, colour, movement, and their several subdivisions, usually with the result of painful and grotesque insistency and onesidedness, from the dreadful bag of bones anatomies of Castagno and Pollaiolo, down to the humbler, but equally necessary, architectural studies of Francesco di Giorgio. Add to this the necessity of uniting the various attainments of such specialists, of taming down these often grotesque monomaniacs, of making all these studies of drawing, anatomy, colour, modelling, perspective, &c., into a picture. If that picture was lacking in individual poetic conception; if those studies were often intolerably silly and wrong-headed from the intellectual point of view; if the old themes were not only worn threadbare, but actually maltreated, what wonder? The themes were there, thank Heaven! no one need bother about them; and no one did. Moreover, as I have already pointed out, no one could have added anything, save in the personal sentiment of the heads, the hands, the tilt of the figure, or the quality of the form. Everything which depends upon dramatic conception, which is not a question of form or sentiment, tended merely to suffer a steady deterioration. Thus, nearly two hundred years after Giotto, Ghirlandaio could find nothing better for his frescoes in St. Trinità than the arrangement of Giotto's St. Francis, with the difference that he omitted all the more delicate dramatic distinctions. I have already alluded to the poetic conception of an early Marriage of the Virgin in the Florence Academy; that essential point of the extreme youth of Mary was never again attended to, although the rest of the arrangement was repeated for two centuries. Similarly, no one noticed or reproduced the delicate distinctions of action which Gaddi had put into his two Annunciations of the Cappella Baroncelli; the shepherds henceforth sprawled no matter how; and the scale of expression in the vision of the Three Kings was not transferred to the more popular theme of their visit to the stable at Bethlehem. In Giotto's Presentation at the Temple in the Arena chapel at Padua, the little Mary is pushed up the steps by her mother; in the Baroncelli frescoes the little girl, ascending gravely, turns round for a minute to bless the children at the foot of the steps. Here are two distinct dramatic conceptions, the one more human, the other more majestic; both admirable. The fifteenth century, nay, the fourteenth, took no account of either; the Virgin merely went up the steps, connected by no emotion with the other characters, a mere little doll, as she is still in the big pictures of Titian and Tintoret, and quite subordinate to any group of richly dressed men or barebacked women. It is difficult to imagine any miracle quite so dull as the Raising of the King's Son in the Brancacci Chapel; its dramatic or undramatic foolishness is surpassed only by certain little panels of Angelico, with fiery rain and other plagues coming down upon the silly blue and pink world of dolls.

A satisfactory study of the lack of all dramatic invention of the painters of the fourteenth and fifteenth centuries is afforded by the various representations of the Annunciation of the Virgin, one of the favourite themes of the early Renaissance. It never seems to have occurred to any one that the Virgin and the Archangel might be displayed otherwise than each in one corner of the picture. Such a composition as that of Rossetti's Ancilla Domini, where the Virgin cowers on her bed as the angel floats in with flames round his feet; such a suggestion as that of the unfinished lily on the embroidery frame, was reserved for our sceptical and irreverent, but imaginative times.

The variety in these Annunciations depends, as I have remarked, not upon a new dramatic conception, producing, as in the case of Rossetti's, a new visible arrangement; but upon the particular kind of form preferred by the artist, and the particular kind of expression common in his pictures; the variety, I may add, is, with one or two exceptions, a variety in inertness. Let us look at a few, taking merely those in one gallery, the Uffizi. The Virgin, in that superb piece of gilding by Simone Martini (did those old painters ever think of the glorified evening sky when they devised such backgrounds?), is turning away from the angel in sheer loathing and anger, a great lady feeling sick at the sudden intrusion of a cad. In a picture by Angelo Gaddi, she is standing with her hand on her chest, just risen from her chair, like a prima donna going to answer an *encore*—a gracious, but not too eager recognition of an expected ovation. In one by Cosimo Rossetti she lifts both hands with shocked astonishment as the angel scuddles in; in the lovely one, with blue Alpine peaks and combed-out hair, now given to Verocchio, she raises one hand with a vacant smile, as if she were exclaiming, "Dear me! there's that angel again." The one slight deviation from the fixed type of Annunciation, Angelico's, in a cell at St. Mark's, where he has made the Virgin kneel and the angel stand, merely because he had painted another Annunciation with a kneeling angel a few doors off, is due to no dramatic inspiration. The angel standing upright with folded arms (how different from Rossetti's standing angel!) while the Virgin kneels, instead of kneeling to her as, according to etiquette, results merely in an impression that this silly, stolid, timid little *Ancilla Domini* (here again one thinks of Rossetti's cowering and dazed Virgin), has been waiting for some time in that kneeling attitude, and that the Archangel has come by appointment.

Among this crowd of unimpressive, nay brainless, representations of one of the grandest and sweetest of all stories, there stand out two—an Annunciation by Signorelli, a small oil painting in the Uffizi, and one by Botticelli,[1] a large tempera picture in the same room. But they stand out merely because the one is the work of the greatest early master of form and movement, or rather the master whose form and movement had a peculiar quality of the colossal; and the other is the work of the man, of all Renaissance painters, whose soul seems to have known most of human, or rather feminine wistfulness, and sorrow, and passion.

The little panel by Signorelli (the lowest compartment, divided into three, of an altar-piece) is perhaps, besides the Orvieto *Resurrection*, his most superb and poetical work. The figures, only three inches high, have his highest quality of powerful grandeur, solemnly rustic in the kneeling shepherds—solemn in the very

[1] Probably executed from Botticelli's design, by Raffaellino del Garbo.

swagger, hand on hip, of the parti-coloured bravoes of the Magi; the landscape, only a few centimetres across, is one of the amplest and most austere that ever has been painted: a valley, bounded by blue hills and dark green ilex groves, wide, silent, inhabited by a race larger and stronger than the human, with more than human passions, but without human speech. In it the Virgin is seated beneath a portico, breathing, as such creatures must breathe, the vast greenness, the deep evening breeze. And to her comes bounding, with waving draperies and loosened hair, the Archangel, like a rushing wind, the wind which the strong woman is quietly inhaling. There is no religious sentiment here, still less any human: the Madonna bows gravely as one who is never astonished; and, indeed, this race of giants, living in this green valley, look as if nothing could ever astonish them—walking miracles themselves, and in constant relation with the superhuman.

We must forget all such things in turning to that Annunciation of Botticelli. The angel has knelt down vehemently, but drawn himself back, frightened at his own message; moved overmuch and awed by what he has to say, and her to whom he must say it; lifting a hand which seems to beg patience, till the speech which is throbbing in his heart can pass his lips; eagerness defeating itself, passionate excitement turned into awe in this young, delicate, passionate, and imaginative creature. He has not said the word; but she has understood. She has seen him before; she knows what he means, this vehement, tongue-tied messenger; and at his sight she reels, her two hands up, the beating of her own blood too loud in her ears, a sudden mist of tears clouding her eyes. This is no simple damsel receiving the message, like Rossetti's terrified and awe-stricken girl, that she is the handmaid of the Lord. This is the nun who has been waiting for years to become Christ's own bride, and receives at length the summons to him, in a tragic overpowering ecstasy, like Catherine in Sodoma's fresco, sinking down at the touch of the rays from Christ's wounds. Nay, this is, in fact, the mere longloving woman, suddenly overcome by the approach of bliss ever hungered for, but never expected, hearing that it is she who is the beloved; and the angel is the knight's squire, excited at the message he has to carry, but terrified at the sight of the woman to whom he must carry it, panting with the weight of another man's love, and learning, as he draws his breath to say those words, what love is himself.

The absence of individual invention, implying the absence of individual dramatic realisation, strikes one more than anywhere in the works of Angelico; and most of all in his frescoes of the cells of St. Mark's. For, while these are evidently less cared for as art, indeed scarcely intended, in their hasty execution, to be considered as paintings at all, they are more strictly religious in intention than any other of Angelico's works; indeed, perhaps, of all paintings in the world, the most exclusively devoted to a religious object,

They are, in fact, so many pages of Scripture stuck up, like texts in a waiting-room, in the cells of the convent: an adjunct to the actual written or printed Bible of each monk. For this reason we expect them to possess what belongs so completely to the German engravers of Dürer's school, the very essential of illustrative art—imaginative realisation of the scenes, an attempt to seize the attention and fill it with the subject. This is by no means the case: for Angelico, although a saint, was a man of the fifteenth century, and, despite all his obvious efforts, he was not a real follower of Giotto. What impressiveness of actual artistic arrangement these frescoes really possess, is due, I think, to no imaginative effort of the artist, but to the exigencies of the place; as any similar impressiveness is due in Signorelli's Annunciation to the quality of his form, and in Botticelli's Annunciation to the pervading character of his heads and gestures. These pale angels and St. Dominicks and Magdalens, these diaphanous, dazzling Christs and Virgins of Angelico's, shining out of the dark corner of the cell made darker, deeper, by the dark green or inky purple ground on which they are painted, are less the spiritual conception of the painter than the accidental result of the darkness of the place, where lines must be simple and colours light, if anything is to be visible. For in the more important frescoes in the corridors and chapter-room, where the light is better, there is a return to Angelico's hackneyed vapid pinks and blues and lilacs, and a return also to his niminy-piminy lines, to all the wax-doll world of the missal painter. The fine fresco of St. Dominick at the foot of the cross, which seems to constitute an exception to this rule, really goes to prove it, since it is intended to be seen very much like the cell frescoes: white and black on a blue ground at the end of the first corridor, a thing to be looked at from a great distance, to impress the lay world that sees it at the cloister and from outside the convent railing. The cell frescoes are, I have said, the most exclusively religious paintings in the world, since they are to the highest degree, what all absolutely pious art must be, *aids to devotion*. Their use is to assist the monk in that conjuring up of the actual momentary feelings, nay, sensations, of the life of Christ which is part of his daily duty. They are such stimuli as the Church has given sometimes in an artistic, sometimes in a literary form, to an imagination jaded by the monotonous contemplation of one subject, or overexcited to the extent of rambling easily to another: they are what we fondly imagine will be the portraits of the dear dead which we place before us, forgetting that after a while we look without seeing, or see without feeling. That this is so, that these painted Gospel leaves stuck on the cell walls are merely such mechanical aids to devotion, explains the curious and startling treatment of some of the subjects, which are yet, despite the seeming novelty and impressiveness, very cold, undramatic, and unimaginative. Thus, there is the fresco of Christ enthroned, blindfold, with alongside of Him a bodiless scoffing head, with hat raised, and in the act of spitting; buffeting hands, equally detached from any body, floating also on the blue background. There is a Christ standing at the foot of the cross, but with his feet in a sarcophagus, the column of the flagellation monumentally or heraldically on one side, the lance of Longinus on the other; and above, to the right, the floating face of Christ being kissed by that of Judas; to the left the blindfold floating head of Christ again, with the floating head of a soldier spitting at Him; and all round buffeting and jibing hands, hands holding the sceptre of reed, and hands counting out money; all arranged very much like the nails, hammer, tweezers and cock on roadside crosses; each a thing whereon to fix the mind, so as to realise that kiss of Judas, that spitting of the soldiers, those slaps; and to hear, if possible, the chink of the pieces of silver that sold our Lord. How different, these two pictorial dodges of the purely mechanical Catholicism of the fifteenth century from the tender or harrowing gospel illustrations, where every detail is conceived as happening in the artist's own town and to his own kinsfolk, of the Lutheran engravers of the school of Dürer!

Thus things go on throughout the fifteenth century, and, indeed, deep into the sixteenth, where traditional arrangement and individual conception overlap, according as a new artistic power does or does not call forth a new dramatic idea. I have already alluded to the fact that the Presentation of the Virgin remains the same, so far as arrangement is concerned, in the pictures of Titian and Tintoret as in the frescoes of Giotto and Gaddi. Michelangelo's Creation of Adam seems still inherited from an obscure painter in the "Green Cloister," who inherited it from the Pisan sculptors. On the other hand, the Resurrection and Last Judgment of Signorelli at Orvieto, painted some years earlier, constitutes in many of its dramatic details a perfectly original work. Be this as it may, and however frequent the recurrence of old themes, with the sixteenth century commences the era of new individual dramatic invention. Michelangelo's Dividing of the Light from the Darkness, where the Creator broods still in chaos, and commands the world to exist; and Raphael's Liberation of St. Peter, with its triple illumination from the moon, the soldier's torches and the glory of the liberating angel, are witnesses that henceforward each man may invent for himself, because each man is in possession of those artistic means which the Giottesques had indicated and the artists of the fifteenth century had laboriously acquired. And now, the Giottesque programme being fulfilled, art may go abroad and seek for new methods and effects, for new dramatic conceptions.

III

The other day, walking along the river near Careggi (with its memories of Lorenzo dei Medici and his Platonists), close to the little cupola and loggia built by Ghirlandaio, I came upon a strip of new grass, thickly whitened with daisies, beneath the poplars beginning to yellow with pale sprouting leaves. And immediately there arose in my mind, by the side of this real grass and real budding of trees, the remembrance of certain early Renaissance pictures: the rusty, green, stencilled grass and flowers of Botticelli, the faded tapestry work of Angelico; making, as it were, the greenness greener, the freshness fresher, of that real grass and those real trees. And not by the force of contrast, but rather by the sense that as all this appears to me green and fresh in the present, so likewise did it appear to those men of four centuries ago: the fact of their having seen and felt, making me, all the more, see and feel.

This is one of the peculiarities of rudimentary art—of the art of the early Renaissance as well as of that of Persia and India, of Constantinople, of every peasant potter all through the world: that, not knowing very well its own aims, it fills its imperfect work with suggestion of all manner of things which it loves, and tries to gain in general pleasurableness what it loses in actual achievement; and lays hold of us, like fragments of verse, by suggestiveness, quite as much as by pictorial realisation. And upon this depends the other half of the imaginative art of the Renaissance, the school of intellectual decoration, of arabesques formed, not of lines and of colours, but of associations and suggestions.

The desire which lies at the bottom of it—a desire masked as religious symbolism in the old mosaicists and carvers and embroiderers—is the desire to paint nice things, in default of painting a fine picture. The beginning of such attempts is naturally connected with the use of gilding; whether those gold grounds of the panel pictures of the fourteenth century represented to the painters only a certain expenditure of gold foil, or whether (as I have suggested, but I fear fantastically) their streakings and veinings of coppery or silvery splendour, their stencillings of rays and dots and fretwork, their magnificent inequality and variety of brown or yellow or greenish effulgence, were vaguely connected in the minds of those men with the splendour of the heaven in which the Virgin and the Saints really dwell. It is the cunning use of this gilding, of tools for ribbing and stencilling and damascening, which give half of their marvellous exotic loveliness to Simone Martini's frescoes at Assisi and his Annunciation of the Florentine Gallery; this, and the feeling for wonderful gold woven and embroidered stuffs, like that white cloth of gold of the kneeling angel, fit, in its purity and splendour, for the robe of Grail king. The want of mechanical dexterity, however, prevented the Giottesques from doing very much in the decorative line except in conjunction with the art—perhaps quite separate from that of the painter, and exercised by a different individual—of the embosser and gilder.

It is with the fifteenth century that begins, in Italy as in Flanders (we must think of the carved stonework, the Persian carpets, the damascened armour, the brocade dresses of Van Eyck's and Memling's Holy Families), the deliberate habit of putting into pictures as much as possible of the beautiful and luxurious things of this world. The house of the Virgin, originally a very humble affair, or rather, in the authority of the early Giottesques, a *no place, nowhere*, develops gradually into a very delightful residence in the choicest part of the town, or into a pleasantly situated villa, like the one described in the Decameron, commanding a fine view. The Virgin's bedchamber, where we are shown it, as, for instance, in Crivelli's picture in the National Gallery, is quite as well appointed in the way of beautiful bedding, carving, and so forth, as the chamber of the lady of John Arnolfini of Lucca in Van Eyck's portrait. Outside it, as we learn from Angelico, Cosimo Rosselli, Lippi, Ghirlandaio, indeed, from almost every Florentine painter, stretches a pleasant portico, decorated in the Ionic or Corinthian style, as if by Brunellesco or Sangallo, with tesselated floor, or oriental carpet, and usually a carved or gilded desk and praying stool; while the privacy of the whole place is guarded by a high wall, surmounted by vases, overtopped by cypresses, and in whose shelter grows a row of well-kept roses and lilies. Sometimes this house, as I have said, becomes a villa, as is the case, not unfrequently, with the Lombards, who love to make the angel appear on the flowery grass against a background of Alpine peaks, such as you see them, rising blue and fairylike from the green ricefields about Pavia. Crivelli, however, though a Lombard, prefers a genteel residence in town, the magnificent Milan of Galeazzo and Filippo Visconti. He gives us a whole street, where richly dressed and well peruked gentlemen look down from the terraces, duly set with flower-pots, of houses ornamented with terra-cotta figures and medallions like those of the hospital at Milan. In this street the angel of the Annunciation is kneeling, gorgeously got up in silks and brocades, and accompanied by a nice little bishop carrying a miniature town on a tray. The Virgin seems to be receiving the message through the window or the open door. She has a beautiful bed with a red silk coverlet, some books, and a shelf covered with plates and preserve jars. This evident appreciation of jam, as one of the pleasant things of this world, corresponds with the pot of flowers on the window, the bird-cage hanging up: the mother of Christ must have the little tastes and luxuries of a well-to-do burgess's daughter. Again, the cell of St. Jerome, painted some thirty years later by Carpaccio, in the Church of the Slavonians, contains not only various convenient and ornamental articles of furniture, but a collection of nick-nacks, among which some antique bronzes are conspicuous.

The charm in all this is not so much that of the actual objects themselves; it is that of their having delighted those people's minds. We are pleased by their pleasure, and our imagination is touched by their fancy. The effect is akin to that of certain kinds of poetry, not the dramatic certainly, where we are pleased by the mere suggestion of beautiful things, and quite as much by finding in the poet a mind appreciative and desirous of them, constantly collecting them and enhancing them by subtle arrangements; it is the case with much lyric verse, with the Italian folk-rhymes, woven out of names of flowers and herbs, with some of Shakespeare's and Fletcher's songs, with the "Allegro" and "Penseroso," Keats, some of Heine, and, despite a mixture of unholy intention, Baudelaire. The great master thereof in the early Renaissance, the lyrist, if I may use the word, of the fifteenth century, is of course Botticelli. He is one of those who most persistently introduce delightful items into their works: elaborately embroidered veils, scarves, and gold fringes. But being a man of fine imagination and most delicate sense of form, he does not, like Angelico or Benozzo or Carpaccio, merely stick pretty things about; he works them all into his strange arabesque, half intellectual, half physical. Thus the screen of roses[1] behind certain of his Madonnas, forming an exquisite Morris

---

[1] I learn from the learned that the Florence and Louvre Madonnas, with the roses, are not Botticelli's; but Botticelli, I am sure, would not have been offended by those lovely bushes being attributed to him.

pattern with the greenish-blue sky interlaced; and those beautiful, carefully-drawn branches of spruce-fir and cypress, lace-like in his Primavera; above all, that fan-like growth of myrtles, delicately cut out against the evening sky, which not merely print themselves as shapes upon the mind, but seem to fill it with a scent of poetry.

This pleasure in the painter's pleasure in beautiful things is connected with another quality, higher and rarer, in this sort of imaginative art. It is our appreciation of the artist's desire for beauty and refinement, of his search for the exquisite. Herein, to my mind, lies some of the secret of Botticelli's fantastic grace; the explanation of that alternate or rather interdependent ugliness and beauty. Botticelli, as I have said elsewhere, must have been an admirer of the grace and sentiment of Perugino, of the delicacy of form of certain Florentine sculptors—Ghiberti, and those who proceed from him, Desiderio, Mino, and particularly the mysterious Florentine sculptor of Rimini; and what these men have done or do, Botticelli attempts, despite or (what is worse) by means of the realistic drawing and ugly models of Florence, the mechanism and arrangement of coarse men like the Pollaiolos. The difficulty of attaining delicate form and sentiment with such materials—it cannot be said to have been attained in that sense by any other early Tuscan painter, not even Angelico or Filippo Lippi—makes the desire but the keener, and turns it into a most persevering and almost morbid research. Thence the extraordinary ingenuity displayed, frequently to the detriment of the work, in the arrangement of hands (witness the tying, clutching hands, with fingers bent curiously in intricate knots, of the Calumny of Apelles), and of drapery; in the poising of bodies and selection of general outline. This search for elegance and grace, for the refined and unhackneyed, is frequently baffled by the ugliness of Botticelli's models, and still more by Botticelli's deficient knowledge of anatomy and habit of good form. But, when not baffled, this desire is extraordinarily assisted by those very defects. This great decorator, who uses the human form as so much pattern element, mere lines and curves like those of a Raffaelesque arabesque, obtains with his imperfect, anatomically defective, and at all events ill-fashioned figures, a far-fetched and poignant grace impossible to a man dealing with more perfect elements. For grace and distinction, which are qualities of movement rather than of form, do not strike us very much in a figure which is originally well made. The momentary charm of movement is lost in the permanent charm of form; the creature could not be otherwise than delightful, made as it is; and we thus miss the sense of selection and deliberate arrangement, the sense of beauty as movement, that is, as grace. Whereas, in the case of defective form, any grace that may be obtained affects us *per se*. It need not have been there; indeed, it was unlikely to be there; and hence it obtains the value and charm of the unexpected, the rare, the far-fetched. This, I think, is the explanation of the something of exotic beauty that attaches to Botticelli: we perceive the structural form only negatively, sufficiently to value all the more the ingenuity of arrangement by which it is made to furnish a beautiful outline and beautiful movement; and we perceive the great desire thereof. If we allow our eye to follow the actual structure of the bodies, even in the Primavera, we shall recognise that not one of these figures but is downright deformed and out of drawing. Even the Graces have arms and shoulders and calves and stomachs all at random; and the most beautiful of them has a slice missing out of her head. But if, instead of looking at heads, arms, legs, bodies, separately, and separate from the drapery, we follow the outline of the groups against the background, drapery clinging or wreathing, arms intertwining, hands combed out into wonderful fingers; if we regard these groups of figures as a pattern stencilled on the background, we recognise that no pattern could be more exquisite in its variety of broken up and harmonised lines. The exquisite qualities of all graceful things, flowers, branches, swaying reeds, and certain animals like the stag and peacock, seem to have been abstracted and given to these half-human and wholly wonderful creatures—these thin, ill put together, unsteady youths and ladies. The ingenious grace of Botticelli passes sometimes from the realm of art to that of poetry, as in the case of those flowers, with stiff, tall stems, which he places by the uplifted foot of the middle Grace, thus showing that she has trodden over it, like Virgil's Camilla, without crushing it. But the element of sentiment and poetry depends in reality upon the fascination of movement and arrangement; fascination seemingly from within, a result of exquisite breeding in those imperfectly made creatures. It is the grace of a woman not beautiful, but well dressed and moving well; the exquisiteness of a song sung delicately by an insufficient or defective voice: a fascination almost spiritual, since it seems to promise a sensitiveness to beauty, a careful avoidance of ugliness, a desire for something more delicate, a reverse of all things gross and accidental, a possibility of perfection.

This imagination of pleasant detail and accessory, which delights us by the intimacy into which we are brought with the artist's innermost conception, develops into what, among the masters of the fifteenth century, I should call the imagination of the fairy tale. A small number of scriptural and legendary stories lend themselves quite particularly to the development of such beautiful accessory, which soon becomes the paramount interest, and vests the whole with a totally new character: a romantic, childish charm, the charm of the improbable taken for granted, of the freedom to invent whatever one would like to see but cannot, the charm of the fairy story. From this unconscious altering of the value of certain Scripture tales, arises a romantic treatment which is naturally applied to all other stories, legends of saints, biographical accounts, Decameronian tales (Mr. Leyland once possessed some Botticellian illustrations of the tale of Nastagio degli Onesti, the hero of Dryden's "Theodore and Honoria," a sort of pendant to the Griseldis attributed to Pinturicchio), and mythological episodes: a new kind of invention, based upon a desire to please, and as different from the invention of the Giottesques as the Arabian Nights are different from Homer.

I have said that it begins with the unconscious altering of the values of certain scriptural stories, owing to the preponderance of detail over accessory. The chief example of this is the Adoration of the Magi. In the paintings of the Giottesques, and in the paintings of the serious, or duller, masters of the fifteenth century—Ghirlandaio, Rosselli, Filippino, those for whom the fairy tale could exist no more than for Michelangelo or Andrea del Sarto—the chief interest in this episode is the Holy Family, the miraculous Babe whom these great folk came so far to see. The fourteenth century made very short work of the kings, allowing them a minimum of splendour; and those of the fifteenth century, who cared only for artistic improvement, copied slavishly, giving the kings their retinue only as they might have introduced any number of studio models or burgesses aspiring at portraits, after the fashion of the Brancacci and S. Maria Novella frescoes, where spectators of miracles make a point never to look at the miraculous proceedings. But there were men who felt differently: the men who loved splendour and detail. To Gentile da Fabriano, that wonderful man in whom begins the colour and romance of Venetian painting,[1] the adoration of the kings could not possibly be what it had been for the Giottesques, or what it still was for Angelico. The Madonna, St. Joseph, the child Christ did not cease to be interesting: he painted them with evident regard, gave the Madonna a beautiful gold hem to her dress, made St. Joseph quite unusually amiable, and shed a splendid gilt glory about the child Christ. But to him the wonderful part of the business was not the family in the shed at Bethlehem which the kings came to see; but those kings themselves, who came from such a long way off. He put himself at the point of view of a holy family less persuaded of its holiness, who should suddenly see a bevy of grand folks come up to their door: the miraculous was here. The spiritual glory was of course on the side of the family of Joseph; but the temporal glory, the glory that delighted Gentile, that went to his brain and made him childishly happy, was with the kings and their retinue. That retinue—the trumpeters prancing on white horses, with gold lace covers, the pages, the armour-bearers, the treasurers, the huntsmen with the hounds, the falconers with the hawks, winding for miles down the

[1] This quality, particularly in the Adoration of the Magi, is already very marked in the very charming and little known frescoes of Ottaviano Nelli, in the former Trinci Palace at Foligno. Nelli was the master of Gentile, and through him greatly influenced Venice.

hills, and expanding into the circle of strange and delightful creatures that kings must have about their persons: jesters with heads thrown back and eyes squeezed close, while thinking of some funny jest; dwarfs and negroes, almost as amusing as their camels and giraffes; tame lynxes chained behind the saddle, monkeys perched, jabbering, on the horses' manes—all this was much more wonderful in Gentile da Fabriano's opinion than all the wonders of the Church, which grew somehow less wonderful the more implicitly you believed in them. Then, in the midst of all these delightful splendours, the kings themselves! The old grey-beard in the brown pomegranate embossed brocade going on all fours, and kissing the little child's feet; the dark young man, with peaked beard and wistful face, removing his coroneted turban; and last, but far from least, the youngest king, the beardless boy, with the complexion of a well-bred young lady, the almond eyes and golden hair, standing up in his tunic of white cloth of silver, while one squire unbuckled his spurs and another removed his cloak. The darling little Prince Charming, between whom and the romantic bearded young king there must for some time have been considerable rivalry, and alternating views in the minds of men and the hearts of women (particularly when the second king, the bearded one, became the John Palæologus of Benozzo), until it was victoriously borne in upon the public that this delicate, beardless creature, so much younger and always the last, must evidently be *the* prince, the youngest of the king's sons in the fairy tales, the one who always succeeds where the two elder have failed, who gets the Water that Dances and the Apple Branch that Sings, who carries off the enchanted oranges, slays the ogre, releases the princess, flies through the air, the hero, the prince of Fairyland. . . .

The fairy business of the story of the Three Kings takes even greater proportions in the delightful frescoes of Benozzo Gozzoli in the Riccardi Chapel. Here the Holy Family are suppressed, so to speak, altogether, tucked into the altar in a picture, and the act of adoration at Bethlehem becomes the mere excuse for the romantic adventures of three people of the highest quality. The journey itself, where Gentile da Fabriano sums up in that procession twisting about the background of his picture, here occupies a whole series of frescoes. And on this journey is concentrated all that the Renaissance knew of splendour, delightfulness, and romance. The green valleys, watered by twisting streams, with matted grasses, which Botticelli puts behind his enthroned Madonna and victorious Judith; Angelico's favourite hillsides with blossoming fruit trees and pointing cypresses; the mysterious firwoods —more mysterious for their remoteness on the high Apennines—which fascinate the fancy of Filippo Lippi; all this is here, and through it all winds the procession of the Three Kings. There are the splendid stuffs and Oriental jewels and trappings, the hounds and monkeys, and jesters and negroes, the falcon on the wrist, the lynxes chained to the saddle, all the magnificence dreamed by Gentile da Fabriano; and among it all ride, met by bevies of peacock-winged angels, kneeling and singing before the flowering rose-hedges, the Three Kings. The old man, who looks like some Platonist philosopher, the beardless prince, surrounded by his noisy huntsmen and pages; and that dark-bearded youth in the Byzantine dress and shovel hat, the genuine king from the East, riding with ardent, wistful eyes, a beautiful kingly young Quixote: Sir Percival seeking the Holy Grail, or King Cophetua seeking for his beggar girl. It is a page of fairy tale, retold by Boiardo or Spenser.

After such things as these it is difficult to speak of those more prosaic tales, really intended as such, on which the painters of the Renaissance spent their fancy. Still they have all their charm, these fairy tales, not of the great poets indeed, but of the nursery.

There is, for instance, the story of a good young man (with a name for a fairy tale too, Æneas Sylvius Piccolomini!) showing his adventures by land and sea and at many courts, the honours conferred on him by kings and emperors, and how at last he was made Pope, having begun as a mere poor scholar on a grey nag; all painted by Pinturicchio in the Cathedral library of Siena. There is the lamentable story of a bride and bridegroom, by Vittore Carpaccio: the stately, tall bride, St. Ursula, and the dear little foolish bridegroom, looking like her little brother; a story containing a great many incidents: the sending of an embassy to the King; the King being sorely puzzled in his mind, leaning his arm upon his bed and asking the Queen's advice; the presence upon the palace steps of an ill-favoured old lady, with a crutch and basket, suspiciously like the bad fairy who had been forgotten at the christening; the apparition of an angel to the Princess, sleeping, with her crown neatly put away at the foot of the bed; the arrival of the big ship in foreign parts, with the Bishop and Clergy putting their heads out of the port-holes and asking very earnestly, "Where are we?" and finally, a most fearful slaughter of the Princess and her eleven thousand ladies-in-waiting. The same Carpaccio—a regular old gossip from whom one would expect all the formulas, "and then he says to the king, Sacred Crown," "and then the Prince walks, walks, walks, walks." "A company of knights in armour nice and shining," "three comely ladies in a green meadow," and so forth of the professional Italian story-teller—the same Carpaccio, who was also, and much more than the more solemn Giovanni Bellini, the first Venetian to handle oil paints like Titian and Giorgione, painted the fairy tale of St. George, with quite the most dreadful dragon's walk, a piece of sea sand embedded with bones and half-gnawed limbs, and crawled over by horrid insects, that any one could wish to see; and quite the most comical dragon, particularly when led out for execution among the minarets and cupolas and camels and turbans and symbols of a kind of small Constantinople.

One of the funniest of all such series of stories, and which shows that when the Renaissance men were driven to it they could still invent, though (apparently) when they had to invent in this fashion, they ceased to be able to paint, is the tale of Griseldis, attributed in our National Gallery to Pinturicchio, but certainly by a very inferior painter of his school. The Marquis, after hunting deer on a steep little hill, shaded by elm trees, sees Griseldis going to a well, a pitcher on her head. He reins in his white horse, and cranes over in his red cloak, the young parti-coloured lords-in-waiting pressing forwards to see her, but only as much as politeness warrants. Scene II.—A stubbly landscape. The Marquis, in red and gold cloak and well-combed yellow head of hair, approaches on foot to the little pink farm-house. Surprise of old Giannucole, who is coming down the exterior steps. "Bless my soul! the Lord Marquis!" "Where is your daughter?" asks the Marquis, with pointing finger. But the daughter, hearing voices, has come on to the balcony and throws up her arms astonished. "Dear me! the cavalier who accosted me in the wood!" The Marquis and Grizel walk off, he deferentially dapper, she hanging back a little in her black smock. Scene III.—The Marquis, still in purple and gold, and red stockings and Hessian boots, says with some timidity and much grace, pointing to the magnificent clothes brought by his courtiers, "Would you mind, dear Grizel, putting on these clothes to please me?" But Griseldis is extremely modest. She tightens her white shift about her, and doesn't dare look at the cloth of gold dress which is so pretty. Scene IV.—A triumphal arch, with four gilt figures. The Marquis daintily, with much wrist-twisting, offers to put the ring on Griseldis' hand, who obediently accepts, while pages and trumpeters hold the Marquis's three horses.

Act II. Scene I.—A portico. Griseldis reluctantly, but obediently, gives up her baby. Scene II.—A conspirator in black cloak and red stockings walks off with it on the tips of his toes, and then returns and tells the Marquis that his Magnificence's orders have been executed. Scene III.—Giannucole, father of Griseldis, having been sent for, arrives in his best Sunday cloak. The Marquis in red, with a crown on, says, standing hand on hip, "You see, after that I really cannot keep her on any longer." Several small dogs sniff at each other in the background. Scene V.—Triumphal arch, with bear chained to it, peacock, tame deer, crowd of courtiers. A lawyer reads the act of divorce. The Marquis steps forward to Grizel with hands raised, "After this kind of behaviour, it is quite impossible for me to live with you any longer." Griseldis is ladylike and resigned. The Marquis says with acrimonious politeness, "I am sorry, madam, I must trouble you to restore to me those garments before departing from my house." Griseldis slowly let her golden frock fall to her feet, then walks off (Scene VI.) towards the little pink farm, where her father is driving the sheep. The courtiers look on and say, "Dear, dear, what very strange things do happen!"

Act III. Scene I.—Outside Giannucole's farm. The Marquis below. Griseldis at the balcony. He says, "I want to hire you as a maid." "Yes, my Lord." Scene II.—A portico, with a large company at dinner. The Marquis introduces his supposed bride and brother-in-law, in reality his own children. He turns round to Griseldis, who is waiting at table, and bids her be a little more careful what she is about with those dishes. Scene III.—Dumb show. Griseldis, in her black smock, is sweeping out the future Marchioness's chamber. Scene IV.—At table. The Marquis suddenly bids Griseldis, who is waiting, come and sit by him; he kisses her, and points at the supposed bride and brother-in-law. "Those are our children, dear." A young footman is quite amazed. Scene V.—A procession of caparisoned horse, and giraffes carrying monkeys. A grand supper. "And they live happy ever after."

But the fairy tale, beyond all others, with these painters of the fifteenth century, is the antique myth. No Bibbienas and Bembos and Calvos have as yet indoctrinated them (as Raphael, alas! was indoctrinated) with the *real spirit of classical times*, teaching them that the essence of antiquity was to have no essence at all; no Ariostos and Tassos have taught the world at large the real Ovidian conception, the monumental allegoric nature and tendency to vacant faces and sprawling, big-toed nudity of the heroes and goddesses as Giulio Romano and the Caracci so well understood to paint them. For all the humanists that hung about courts, the humanities had not penetrated much into the Italian people. The imaginative form and colour was still purely mediæval; and the artists of the early Renaissance had to work out their Ovidian stories for themselves, and work them out of their own material. Hence the mythological creatures of these early painters are all, more or less, gods in exile, with that charm of a long residence in the Middle Ages which makes, for instance, the sweetheart of Ritter Tannhäuser so infinitely more seductive than the paramour of Adonis; that charm which, when we meet it occasionally in literature, in parts of Spenser, for instance, or in a play like Peel's "Arraignment of Paris," is so peculiarly delightful.

These early painters have made up their Paganism for themselves, out of all pleasant things they knew; their fancy has brooded upon it; and the very details that make us laugh, the details coming direct from the Middle Ages, the spirit in glaring opposition occasionally to that of Antiquity, bring home to us how completely this Pagan fairyland is a genuine reality to these men. We feel this in nearly all the work of that sort—least, in the archæological Mantegna's. We see it beginning in the mere single figures—the various drawings of Orpheus, "Orpheus le doux menestrier jouant de flutes et de musettes," as Villon called him, much about that time—piping or fiddling among little toy animals out of a Nuremberg box; the drawing of fauns carrying sheep, some with a queer look of the Good Shepherd about them, of Pinturicchio; and rising to such wonderful exhibitions (to me, with their obscure reminiscence of pageants, they always seem like ballets) as Perugino's Ceiling of the Cambio, where, among arabesqued constellations, the gods of antiquity move gravely along: the bearded knight Mars, armed *cap-à-pie* like a mediæval warrior; the delicate Mercurius, a beautiful page-boy stripped of his emblazoned clothes; Luna dragged along by two nymphs; and Venus daintily poised on one foot on her dove-drawn chariot, the exquisite Venus in her clinging veils, conquering the world with the demure gravity and adorable primness of a high-born young abbess.

The actual fairy story becomes, little by little, more complete—the painters of the fifteenth century work, little guessing it, are the precursors of Walter Crane. The full-page illustration of a tale of semi-mediæval romance—of a romance like Spenser's "Fairy Queen" or Mr. Morris's "Earthly Paradise," exists distinctly in that picture and drawing, by the young Raphael or whomsoever else, of Apollo and Marsyas.[1] This piping Marsyas seated by the tree stump, this naked Apollo, thin and hectic like an undressed archangel, standing against the Umbrian valley with its distant blue hills,

[1] I believe now unanimously given to Pinturicchio.

its castellated village, its delicate, thinly-leaved trees—things we know so well in connection with the Madonna and Saints, that this seems absent for only a few minutes—all this is as little like Ovid as the triumphant antique Galatea of Raphael is like Spenser. Again, there is Piero di Cosimo's Death of Procris: the poor young woman lying dead by the lake, with the little fishing town in the distance, the swans sailing and cranes strutting, and the dear young faun—no Praxitelian god with invisible ears, still less the obscene beast whom the late Renaissance copied from Antiquity—a most gentle, furry, rustic creature, stooping over her in puzzled, pathetic concern, at a loss, with his want of the practice of cities and the knowledge of womankind, what to do for this poor lady lying among the reeds and the flowering scarlet sage; a creature the last of whose kind (friendly, shy, woodland things, half bears or half dogs, frequent in mediæval legend), is the satyr of Fletcher's "Faithful Shepherdess," the only poetic conception in that gross and insipid piece of magnificent rhetoric. The perfection of the style must naturally be sought from Botticelli, and in his Birth of Venus (but who may speak of that after the writer of most subtle fancy, of most exquisite language, among living Englishman?) [1] This goddess, not triumphant but sad in her pale beauty,

---

[1] Alas! no longer among the living, though among those whose spiritual part will never die. Walter Pater died July 1894: a man whose sense of loveliness and dignity made him, in mature life, as learned in moral beauty as he had been in visible.

a king's daughter bound by some charm to flit on her shell over the rippling sea, until the winds blow it in the kingdom of the good fairy Spring, who shelters her in her laurel grove and covers her nakedness with the wonderful mantle of fresh-blown flowers. . . .

But the imagination born of the love of beautiful and suggestive detail soars higher; become what I would call the lyric art of the Renaissance, the art which not merely gives us beauty, but stirs up in ourselves as much beauty again of stored-up impression, reaches its greatest height in certain Venetian pictures of the early sixteenth century. Pictures of vague or enigmatic subject, or no subject at all, like Giorgione's Fête Champêtre and Soldier and Gipsy, Titian's Sacred and Profane Love, The Three Ages of Man, and various smaller pictures by Bonifazio, Palma, Basaiti; pictures of young men in velvets and brocades, solemn women with only the glory of their golden hair and flesh, seated in the grass, old men looking on pensive, children rolling about; with the solemnity of great, spreading trees, of greenish evening skies; the pathos of the song about to begin or just finished, lute or viol or pipe still lying hard by. Of such pictures it is best, perhaps, not to speak. The suggestive imagination is wandering vaguely, dreaming; fumbling at random sweet, strange chords out of its viol, like those young men and maidens. The charm of such works is that they are never explicit; they tell us, like music, deep secrets, which we feel, but cannot translate into words.

IV

The first new factor in art which meets us at the beginning of the sixteenth century is not among the Italians, and is not a merely artistic power. I speak of the passionate individual fervour for the newly recovered Scriptures, manifest among the German engravers, Protestants all or nearly all, and among whose works is for ever turning up the sturdy, passionate face of Luther, the enthusiastic face of Melanchthon. The very nature of these men's art is conceivable only where the Bible has suddenly become the reading, and the chief reading, of the laity. These prints, large and small, struck off in large numbers, are not church ornaments like frescoes or pictures, nor aids to monastic devotion like Angelico's Gospel histories at St. Mark's —they are illustrations to the book which every one is reading, things to be framed in the chamber of every burgher or mechanic, to be slipped into the prayer-book of every housewife, to be conned over during the long afternoons, by the children near the big stove or among the gooseberry bushes of the garden. And they are, therefore, much more than the Giottesque inventions, the expression of the individual artist's ideas about the incidents of Scripture; and an expression not for the multitude at large, fresco or mosaic that could be elaborated by a sceptical or godless artist, but a re-explanation as from man to man and friend: this is how the dear Lord looked, or acted—see, the words in the Bible are so or so forth. Therefore, there enters into these designs, which contain after all only the same sort of skill which was rife in Italy, so much homeliness at once, and poignancy and sublimity of imagination. The Virgin, they have discovered, is not that grandly dressed lady, always in the very finest brocade, with the very finest manners, and holding a divine infant that has no earthly wants, whom Van Eyck and Memling and Meister Stephan painted. She is a good young woman, a fairer version of their dear wife, or the woman who might have been that; no carefully selected creature as with the Italians, no well-made studio model, with figure unspoilt by child-bearing, but a real wife and mother, with real milk in her breasts (the Italian virgin, save with one or two Lombards, is never permitted to suckle)[1], which she very readily and thoroughly gives to the child, guiding the little mouth with her fingers. And she sits in the lonely fields by the hedges and windmills in the fair weather; or in the neat little chamber with the walled town visible between the pillar of the window, as in Bartholomew Beham's exquisite design, reading, or suckling, or sewing, or soothing the fretful baby; no angels around her, or rarely: the Scripture says nothing about such a court of seraphs as the Italians and Flemings, the superstitious Romanists, always placed round the mother

[1] And the circular so-called Botticelli (now given, I believe, to San Gallo) in the National Gallery.

of Christ. It is all as it might have happened to them; they translate the Scripture into their everyday life, they do not pick out of it the mere stately and poetic incidents like the Giottesques. This everyday life of theirs is crude enough, and in many cases nasty enough; they have in those German free towns a perfect museum of loathsome ugliness, born of ill ventilation, gluttony, starvation, or brutality: quite fearful wrinkled harridans and unabashed fat, guzzling harlots, and men of every variety of scrofula, and wart and belly, towards none of which (the best far transcending the worst Italian Judas) they seem to feel any repugnance. They have also a beastly love of horrors; their decollations and flagellations are quite sickening in detail, as distinguished from the tidy, decorous executions of the early Italians; and one feels that they do enjoy seeing, as in one of their prints, the bowels of St. Erasmus being taken out with a windlass, or Jael, as Altdorfer has shown her in his romantic print, neatly hammering the nail into the head of the sprawling, snoring Sisera. There is a good deal of grossness, too (of which, among the Italians, even Robetta and similar, there is so little), in the details of village fairs and adventures of wenches with their Schatz; and a strange permeating nightmare, gruesomeness of lewd, warty devils, made up of snouts, hoofs, bills, claws, and incoherent parts of incoherent creatures; of perpetual skeletons climbing in trees, or appearing behind flower-beds. But there is also—and Holbein's Dance of Death, terrible, jocular, tender, vulgar and poetic, contains it all, this German world—a great tenderness. Tenderness not merely in the heads of women and children, in the fervent embrace of husband and wife and mother and daughter; but in the feeling for dumb creatures and inanimate things, the gentle dogs of St. Hubert, the deer that crouch among the rocks with Genevieve, the very tangled grasses and larches and gentians that hang to the crags, drawn as no Italian ever drew them; the quiet, sentimental little landscapes of castles on fir-clad hills, of manor-houses, gabled and chimneyed, among the reeds and willows of shallow ponds. These feelings, Teutonic doubtless, but less mediæval than we might think, for the Middle Ages of the Minnesingers were terribly conventional, seem to well up at the voice of Luther; and it is this which make the German engravers, men not always of the highest talents, invent new and beautiful Gospel pictures. Of these I would take two as typical—typical of individual fancy most strangely contrasting with the conventionalism of the Italians. Let the reader think of any of the scores of Flights into Egypt, and of Resurrections by fifteenth-century Italians, or even Giottesques; and then turn to two prints, one of each of these subjects respectively, by Martin Schongauer and Altdorfer. Schongauer gives a delightful oasis: palms and prickly pears, the latter conceived as growing at the top of a tree; below, lizards at play and deer grazing; in this place the

Virgin has drawn up her ass, who browses the thistles at his feet, while St. Joseph, his pilgrim bottle bobbing on his back, hangs himself with all his weight to the branches of a date palm, trying to get the fruit within reach. Meanwhile a bevy of sweet little angels have come to the rescue; they sit among the branches, dragging them down towards him, and even bending the whole stem at the top so that he may get at the dates. Such a thing as this is quite lovely, particularly after the routine of St. Joseph trudging along after the donkey, the eternal theme of the Italians. In Altdorfer's print Christ is ascending in a glory of sunrise clouds, banner in hand, angels and cherubs peering with shy curiosity round the cloud edge. The sepulchre is open, guards asleep or stretching themselves, and yawning all round; and childish young angels look reverently into the empty grave, rearranging the cerecloths, and trying to roll back the stone lid. One of them leans forward, and utterly dazzles a negro watchman, stepping forward, lantern in hand; in the distance shepherds are seen prowling about. "This," says Altdorfer to himself, "is how it must have happened."

Hence, among these Germans, the dreadful seriousness and pathos of the Passion, the violence of the mob, the brutality of the executioners, above all, the awful sadness of Christ. There is here somewhat of the realisation of what He must have felt in finding the world He had come to redeem so vile and cruel. In what way, under what circumstances, such thoughts would come to these men, is revealed to us by that magnificent head of the suffering Saviour—a design apparently for a carved crucifix—under which Albrecht Dürer wrote the pathetic words: " I drew this in my sickness."

Thus much of the power of that new factor, the individual interest in the Scriptures. All other innovations on the treatment of religious themes were due, in the sixteenth century, but still more in the seventeenth, to the development of some new artistic possibility, or to the gathering together in the hands of one man of artistic powers hitherto existing only in a dispersed condition. This is the secret of the greatness of Raphael as a pictorial poet, that he could do all manner of new things merely by holding all the old means in his grasp. This is the secret of those wonderful inventions of his, which do not take our breath away like Michelangelo's or Rembrandt's, but seem at the moment the one and only right rendering of the subject: the Liberation of St. Peter, Heliodorus, Ezechiel, and the whole series of magnificent Old Testament stories on the ceiling of the Loggie. In Raphael we see the perfect fulfilment of the Giottesque programme: he can do all that the first theme inventors required for the carrying out of their ideas; and therefore he can have new, entirely new, themes. Raphael furnishes, for the first time since Giotto, an almost complete set of pictorial interpretations of Scripture.

We are now, as we proceed in the sixteenth century, in the region where new artistic powers admit of new imaginative conceptions on the part of the individual. We gain immensely by the liberation from the old tradition, but we lose immensely also. We get the benefit of the fancy and feelings of this individual, but we are at the mercy, also, of his stupidity and vulgarity. Of this the great examples are Tintoretto, and after him Velasquez and Rembrandt. Of Tintoret I would speak later, for he is eminently the artist in whom the gain and the loss are most typified, and perhaps most equally distributed, and because, therefore, he contrasts best with the masters anterior to Raphael.

The new powers in Velasquez and Rembrandt were connected with the problem of light, or rather, one might say, in the second case, of darkness. This new faculty of seizing the beauties, momentary and not inherent in the object, due to the various effects of atmosphere and lighting up, added probably a good third to the pleasure-bestowing faculty of art; it was the beginning of a kind of democratic movement against the stern domination of such things as were privileged in shape and colour. A thousand things, ugly or un-imaginative in themselves, a plain face, a sallow complexion, an awkward gesture, a dull arrangement of lines, could be made delightful and suggestive. A wet yard, a pail and mop, and a servant washing fish under a pump could become, in the hands of Peter de Hoogh, and thanks to the magic of light and shade, as beautiful and interesting in their way as a swirl of angels and lilies by Botticelli. But this redemption of the vulgar was at the expense, as I have elsewhere pointed out, of a certain growing callousness to vulgarity. What holds good as to the actual artistic, visible quality, holds good also as to the imaginative value. Velasquez's Flagellation, if indeed it be his, in our National Gallery, has a pathos, a something that catches you by the throat, in that melancholy weary body, broken with ignominy and pain, sinking down by the side of the column, which is inseparable from the dreary grey light, the livid colour of the flesh—there is no joy in the world where such things can be. But the angel who has just entered has not come from heaven—such a creature is fit only to roughly shake up the pillows of paupers, dying in the damp dawn in the hospital wards.

It is, in a measure, different with Rembrandt, exactly because he is the master, not of light, but of darkness, or of light that utterly dazzles. His ugly women and dirty Jews of Rotterdam are either hidden in the gloom or reduced to mere vague outlines, specks like gnats in the sunshine, in the effulgence of light. Hence we can enjoy, almost without any disturbing impressions, the marvellous imagination shown in his etchings of Bible stories. Rembrandt is to Dürer as an archangel to a saint: where the German draws, the Dutchman seems to bite his etching plate with elemental darkness and glory. Of these etchings I would mention a few; the reader may put these indications alongside of his remembrances of the Arena Chapel, or of Angelico's cupboard panels in the Academy at Florence: they show how intimately dramatic imagination depends in art upon mere technical means, how hopelessly limited to mere indication were the early artists, how forced along the path of dramatic realisation are the men of modern times.

The Annunciation to the Shepherds: The heavens open in a circular whirl among the storm darkness, cherubs whirling distantly like innumerable motes in a sunbeam; the angel steps forward on a ray of light, projecting into the ink-black night. The herds have perceived the vision, and rush headlong in all directions, while the trees groan beneath the blast of that opening of heaven. A horse, seen in profile, with the light striking on his eyeball, seems paralysed by terror. The shepherds have only just awakened. *The Nativity:* Darkness. A vague crowd of country folk jostling each other noiselessly. A lantern, a white speck in the centre, sheds a smoky, uncertain light on the corner where the Child sleeps upon the pillows, the Virgin, wearied, resting by its side, her face on her hand. Joseph is seated by, only his head visible above his book. The cows are just visible in the gloom. The lantern is held by a man coming carefully forward, uncovering his head, the crowd behind him. *A Halt on the Journey to Egypt:* Night. The lantern hung on a branch. Joseph seated sleepily, with his fur cap drawn down; the Virgin and Child resting against the packsaddle on the ground. *An Interior:* The Virgin hugging and rocking the Child. Joseph, outside, looks in through the window. *The Raising of Lazarus:* A vault hung with scimitars, turbans, and quivers. Against the brilliant daylight just let in, the figure of Christ, seen from behind, stands out in His long robes, raising His hand to bid the dead arise. Lazarus, pale, ghost-like in this effulgence, slowly, wearily raises his head in the sepulchre. The crowd falls back. Astonishment, awe. This coarse Dutchman has suppressed the incident of the bystanders holding their nose, to which the Giottesques clung desperately. This is not a moment to think of stenches or infection. *Entombment:* Night. The platform below the cross. A bier, empty, spread with a winding-sheet, an old man arranging it at the head. The dead Saviour being slipped down from the cross on a sheet, two men on a ladder letting the body down, others below receiving it, trying to prevent the arm from trailing. Immense solemnity, carefulness, hushedness. A distant illuminated palace blazes out in the night. One feels that they are stealing Him away.

I have reversed the chronological order and chosen to speak of Tintoret after Rembrandt, because, being an Italian and still in contact with some of the old tradition, the great Venetian can show more completely, both what was gained and what was lost in imaginative rendering by the liberation of the individual artist and the development of artistic means. First, of the gain. This depends mainly upon Tintoret's handling of light and shade, and his foreshortenings: it enables him to compose entirely in huge masses, to divide or concentrate the interest, to throw into vague insignificance the less important parts of a situation in order to insist upon the more important; it gives him the power also of impressing us by the colossal and the ominous. The masterpiece of this style, and probably Tintoret's masterpiece therefore, is the great Crucifixion at S. Rocco. To feel its full tragic splendour one must think of the finest things which the early Renaissance achieved, such as Luini's beautiful fresco at Lugano; by the side of the painting at S. Rocco everything is tame, except, perhaps, Rembrandt's etching called the Three Crosses. After this, and especially to be compared with the frescoes of Masaccio and Ghirlandaio of the same subject, comes the Baptism of Christ. The old details of figures dressing and undressing, which gave so much pleasure to earlier painters, for instance, Piero della Francesca, in the National Gallery, are entirely omitted, as the nose-holding in the Raising of Lazarus, is omitted by Rembrandt. Christ kneels in the Jordan, with John bending over him, and vague multitudes crowding the banks, distant, dreamlike beneath the yellow stormlight. Of Tintoret's Christ before Pilate, of that figure of the Saviour, long, straight, wrapped in white and luminous like his own wraith, I have spoken already. But I must speak of the S. Rocco Christ in the Garden, as imaginative as anything by Rembrandt, and infinitely more beautiful. The moonlight tips the draperies of the three sleeping apostles, gigantic, solemn. Above, among the bushes, leaning His head on His hand, is seated Christ, weary to death, numbed by grief and isolation, recruiting for final resistance. The sense of being abandoned of all men and of God has never been brought home in this way by any other painter; the little tear-stained Saviours, praying in broad daylight, of Perugino and his fellows, are mere distressed mortals. This betrayed and resigned Saviour has upon Him the *weltschmerz* of Prometheus. But even here we begin to feel the loss, as well as the gain, of the painter being forced from the dramatic routine of earlier days: instead of the sweet, tearful little angel of the early Renaissance, there comes to this tragic Christ, in a blood-red nimbus, a brutal winged creature thrusting the cup in His face. The uncertainty of Tintoret's inspirations, the uncertainty of result of these astonishing pictorial methods of attaining the dramatic, the occasional vapidness and vulgarity of the man, unrestrained by any stately tradition like the vapidness and vulgarity of so many earlier masters,[1] comes out already at S. Rocco. And principally in the scene of

---

[1] How peccable is the individual imagination, unchastened by tradition! I find among the illustrations of Mr. Berenson's very valuable monograph on Lotto, a most curious instance in point. This psychological, earnest painter has been betrayed, by his morbid nervousness of temper, into making the starting of a cat into the second most important incident in his Annunciation.

the Temptation, a theme rarely, if ever, treated before the sixteenth century, and which Tintoret has made unspeakably mean in its unclean and dramatically impotent suggestiveness: the Saviour parleying from a kind of rustic edifice with a good-humoured, fat, half feminine Satan, fluttering with pink wings like some smug seraph of Bernini's pupils. After this it is scarce necessary to speak of whatever is dramatically abortive (because successfully expressing just the wrong sort of sentiment, the wrong situation) in Tintoret's work: his Woman taken in Adultery, with the dapper young Rabbi, offended neither by adultery in general nor by this adulteress in particular; the Washing of the Feet, in London, where the conversation appears to turn upon the excessive hotness or coldness of the water in the tub; the Last Supper at S. Giorgio Maggiore, where, among the mysterious wreaths of smoke peopled with angels, Christ rises from His seat and holds the cup to His neighbour's lips with the gesture, as He says, "This is My blood," of a conjuror to an incredulous and indifferent audience. To Tintoret the contents of the chalice is the all-important matter: where is the majesty of the old Giottesque gesture, preserved by Leonardo, of pushing forward the bread with one hand, the wine with the other, and thus uncovering the head and breast of the Saviour, the gesture which does indeed mean—"I am the bread you shall eat, and the wine you shall drink"? There remains, however, to mention another work of Tintoret's which, coming in contact with one's recollections of earlier art, may suggest strange doubts and wellnigh shake one's faith in the imaginative efficacy of all that went before: his enormous canvas of the Last Day, at S. Maria dell' Orto. The first and overwhelming impression, even before one has had time to look into this apocalyptic work, is that no one could have conceived such a thing in earlier days, not even Michelangelo when he painted his Last Judgment, nor Raphael when he designed the Vision of Ezechiel. This is, indeed, one thinks, a revelation of the end of all things. Great storm clouds, whereon throne the Almighty and His Elect, brood over the world, across which, among the crevassed, upheaving earth, pours the wide glacier torrent of Styx, with the boat of Charon struggling across its precipitous waters. The angels, confused with the storm clouds of which they are the spirit, lash the damned down to the Hell stream, band upon band, even from the far distance. And in the foreground the rocks are splitting, the soil is upheaving with the dead beneath; here protrudes a huge arm, there a skull; in one place the clay, rising, has assumed the vague outline of the face below. In the rocks and water, among the clutching, gigantic men, the huge, full-bosomed woman, tosses a frightful half-fleshed carcass, grass still growing from his finger tips, his grinning skull, covered half with hair and half with weeds, greenish and mouldering: a sinner still green in earth and already arising.

A wonderful picture: a marvellous imaginative mind, with marvellous imaginative means at his command. Yet, let us ask ourselves, what is the value of the result? A magnificent display of attitudes and forms, a sort of bravura ghastliness and impressiveness, which are in a sense *barrocco*, reminding us of the wax plague models of Florence and of certain poems of Baudelaire's. But of the feeling, the poetry of this greatest of all scenes, what is there? And, standing before it, I think instinctively of that chapel far off on the windswept Umbrian rock, with Signorelli's Resurrection: a flat wall accepted as a flat wall, no place, nowhere. A half-dozen groups, not closely combined. Colour reduced to monochrome; light and shade nowhere, as nowhere also all these devices of perspective. But in that simply treated fresco, with its arrangement as simple as that of a vast antique bas-relief, there is an imaginative suggestion far surpassing this of Tintoret's. The breathless effort of the youths breaking through the earth's crust, shaking their long hair and gasping; the stagger of those rising to their feet; the stolidity, hand on hip, of those who have recovered their body but not their mind, blinded by the light, deafened by the trumpets of Judgment; the absolute self-abandonment of those who can raise themselves no higher; the dull, awe-stricken look of those who have found their companions, clasping each other in vague, weak wonder; and further, under the two archangels who stoop downwards with the pennons of their trumpets streaming in the blast, those figures who beckon to the re-found beloved ones, or who shade their eyes and point to a glory on the horizon, or who, having striven forward, sink on their knees, overcome by a vision which they alone can behold. And recollecting that fresco of Signorelli's, you feel as if this vast, tall canvas at S. Maria dell' Orto, where topple and welter the dead and the quick, were merely so much rhetorical rhodomontade by the side of the old hymn of the Last Day—

> "Mors stupebit et natura
> Quum resurget creatura
> Judicanti responsura."

V

Again, in the chaos of newly-developing artistic means, and of struggling individual imaginations, we get once more, at the end of the eighteenth century, to what we found at the beginning of the fourteenth: the art that does not show, but merely speaks. We find it in what, of all things, are the apparently most different to the quiet and placid outline illustration of the Giottesque: in the terrible portfolio of Goya's etchings, called the Disasters of War. Like Dürer and Rembrandt, the great Spaniard is at once extremely realistic and extremely imaginative. But his realism means fidelity, not to the real aspect of things, of the *thing in itself*, so to speak, but to the way in which things will appear to the spectator at a given moment. He isolates what you might call a case, separating it from the multitude of similar cases, giving you one execution where several must be going on, one firing off of cannon, one or two figures in a burning or a massacre; and his technique conduces thereunto, blurring a lot, rendering only the outline and gesture, and that outline and gesture frequently so momentary as to be confused. But he is real beyond words in his reproduction of the way in which such dreadful things must stamp themselves upon the mind. They are isolated, concentrated, distorted: the multiplicity of horrors making the perceiving mind more sensitive, morbid as from opium eating, and thus making the single impression, which excludes all the rest, more vivid and tremendous than, without that unconsciously perceived rest, it could possibly be. Nay, more, these scenes are not merely rather such as they were recollected than as they really were seen; they are such as they were recollected in the minds and feelings of peasants and soldiers, of people who could not free their attention to arrange all these matters logically, to give them their relative logical value. The slaughtering soldiers—Spaniards, English, or French—of the Napoleonic period become in his plates Turks, Saracens, huge vague things in half Oriental costumes, whiskered, almost turbaned in their fur caps, they become almost ogres, even as they must have done in the popular mind. The shooting of deserters and prisoners is reduced to the figures at the stake, the six carbine muzzles facing them: no shooting soldiers, no stocks to the carbines, any more than in the feeling of the man who was being shot. The artistic training, the habit of deliberately or unconsciously looking for visible effects which all educated moderns possess, prevents even our writers from thus reproducing what has been the actual mental reality. But Goya does not for a moment let us suspect the presence of the artist, the quasi-writer. The impression reproduced is the impression, not of the artistic bystander, but of the sufferer or the sufferer's comrades. This makes him extraordinarily faithful to the epigraphs of his plates. We feel that the woman, all alone, without bystanders, earthworks, fascines, smoke, &c., firing off the cannon, is the woman as she is remembered by the creature who exclaims, "Que valor!" We feel that the half-dead soldier being stripped, the condemned turning his head aside as far as the rope will permit, the man fallen crushed beneath his horse or vomiting out his blood, is the wretch who exclaims, "Por 'eso soy nacido!" They are, these etchings of Goya's, the representation of the sufferings, real and imaginative, of the real sufferers. In the most absolute sense they are the art which does not merely show, but tells; the suggestive and dramatic art of the individual, unaided and unhampered by tradition, indifferent to form and technicality, the art which even like the art of the immediate predecessors of Giotto, those Giuntas and Berlinghieris, who left us the hideous and terrible Crucifixions, says to the world, "You shall understand and feel."

TUSCAN SCULPTURE

I

WE are all of us familiar with the two adjacent rooms at South Kensington which contain, respectively, the casts from antique sculpture and those from the sculpture of the Renaissance; and we are familiar also with the sense of irritation or of relief which accompanies our passing from one of them to the other. This feeling is typical of our frame of mind towards various branches of the same art, and, indeed, towards all things which might be alike, but happen to be unlike. Times, countries, nations, temperaments, ideas, and tendencies, all benefit and suffer alternately by our habit of considering that if two things of one sort are not identical, one must be in the right and the other in the wrong. The act of comparison evokes at once our innate tendency to find fault; and having found fault, we rarely perceive that, on better comparing, there may be no fault at all to find.

As the result of such comparison, we shall find that Renaissance sculpture is unrestful, huddled, lacking selection of form and harmony of proportions; it reproduces uglinesss and perpetuates effort; it is sometimes grotesque, and frequently vulgar. Or again, that antique sculpture is conventional, insipid, monotonous, without perception for the charm of detail or the interest of individuality; afraid of movement and expression, and at the same time indifferent to outline and grouping; giving us florid nudities which never were alive, and which are doing and thinking nothing whatever. Thus, according to which room or which mood we enter first, we are sure to experience either irritation at wrong-headedness or relief at right-doing; whether we pass from the sculpture of ancient Greece to the sculpture of mediæval Italy, or *vice versâ*.

But a more patient comparison of these two branches of sculpture, and of the circumstances which made each what it was, will enable us to enjoy the very different merits of both, and will teach us also something of the vital processes of the particular spiritual organism which we call an art.

In the early phase of the philosophy of art—a phase lingering on to our own day in the works of certain critics—the peculiarities of a work of art were explained by the peculiarities of character of the artist: the paintings of Raphael and the music of Mozart partook of the gentleness of their life; while the figures of Michelangelo and the compositions of Beethoven were the outcome of their misanthropic ruggedness of temper. The insufficiency, often the falseness, of such explanations became evident when critics began to perceive that the works of one time and country usually possessed certain common peculiarities which did not correspond to any resemblance between the characters of their respective artists; peculiarities so much more dominant than any others, that a statue or a picture which was unsigned and of obscure history was constantly attributed to half-a-dozen contemporary sculptors or painters by half-a-dozen equally learned critics. The recognition of this fact led to the substitution of the *environment* (the *milieu* of Monsieur Taine) as an explanation of the characteristics, no longer of a single work of art, but of a school or group of kindred works. Greek art henceforth was the serene outcome of a serene civilisation of athletes, poets, and philosophers, living with untroubled consciences in a good climate, with slaves and helots to char for them while they ran races, discussed elevated topics, and took part in Panathenaic processions, riding half naked on prancing horses, or carrying olive branches and sacrificial vases in honour of a divine patron, in whom they believed only as much as they liked. And the art of the Middle Ages was the fantastic, far-fetched, and often morbid production of nations of crusaders and theologians, burning heretics, worshipping ladies, seeing visions, and periodically joining hands in a vertiginous death-reel, whose figures were danced from country to country. This new explanation, while undoubtedly less misleading than the other one, had the disadvantage of straining the characteristics of a civilisation or of an art in order to tally with its product or producer; it forgot that Antiquity was not wholly represented by the frieze of the Parthenon, and that the Gothic cathedrals and the frescoes of Giotto had characteristics more conspicuous than morbidness and insanity.

Moreover, in the same way that the old personal criticism was unable to account for the resemblance between the works of different individuals of the same school, so the theory of the environment fails to explain certain qualities possessed in common by various schools of art and various arts which have arisen under the pressure of different civilisations; and it is obliged to slur over the fact that the sculpture of the time of Pericles and Alexander, the painting of the early sixteenth century, and the music of the age of Handel, Haydn, and Mozart are all very much more like one another in their serene beauty than they are any of them like the other productions, artistic or human, of their environment. Behind this explanation there must therefore be another, not controverting the portion of truth it contains, but completing it by the recognition of a relation more intimate than that of the work of art with its environment: the relation of form and material. The perceptions of the artist, what he sees and how he sees it, can be transmitted to others only through processes as various as themselves: hair seen as colour is best imitated with paint, hair seen as form with twisted metal wire. It is as impossible to embody certain perceptions in some stages of handicraft as it would be to construct a complex machine in a rudimentary condition of mechanics. Certain modes of vision require certain methods of painting, and these require certain kinds of surface and pigment. Until these exist, a man may see correctly, but he cannot reproduce what he is seeing. In short, the work of art represents the meeting of a mode of seeing and feeling (determined partly by individual characteristics, partly by those of the age and country) and of a mode of treating materials, a craft which may itself be, like the mind of the artist, in a higher or lower stage of development.

The early Greeks had little occasion to become skilful carvers of stone. Their buildings, which reproduced a very simple wooden structure, were ornamented with little more than the imitation of the original carpentering; for the Ionic order, poor as it is of ornament, came only later; and the Corinthian, which alone offered scope for variety and skill of carving, arose only when figure sculpture was mature. But the Greeks, being only just in the iron period (and iron, by the way, is the tool for stone), were great moulders of clay and casters of metal. The things which later ages made of iron, stone, or wood, they made of clay or bronze. The thousands of exquisite utensils, weapons, and toys in our museums make this apparent; from the bronze greaves delicately modelled like the legs they were to cover, to the earthenware dolls, little Venuses, exquisitely dainty, with articulated legs and go-carts.

Hence the human figure came to be imitated by a process which was not sculpture in the literal sense of carving. It is significant that the Latin word whence we get *effigy* has also given us *fictile*, the making of statues being thus connected with the making of pots; and that the whole vocabulary of ancient authors shows that they thought of statuary not as akin to cutting and chiselling, but to moulding ($\pi\lambda\acute{a}\sigma\sigma\omega =$ *fingo*), shaping out of clay on the wheel or with the modelling tool.[1] It seems probable that marble-work was but rarely used for the round until the sixth century; and the treatment of the hair, the propping of projecting limbs and drapery, makes it obvious that a large proportion of the antiques in our possession are marble copies of long-destroyed bronzes.[2] So that the Greek statue, even if eventually destined for marble, was conceived by a man having the habit of modelling in clay.

Let us turn from early Greece to mediæval Italy. Hammered iron had superseded bronze for weapons and armour, and silver and gold, worked with the chisel, for ornaments. On the other hand, the introduction from the East of glazed pottery had banished

[1] I am confirmed in these particulars by my friend Miss Eugenie Sellers, whose studies of the ancient authorities on art—Lucian, Pausanias, Pliny, and others, will be the more fruitful that they are associated with knowledge—uncommon in archæologists—of more modern artistic processes.

[2] This becomes overwhelmingly obvious on reading Professor Furtwängler's great "Masterpieces of Greek Sculpture." Praxiteles appears to have been exceptional in his preference for marble.

to the art of the glass-blower all fancy in shaping utensils. There was no demand in common life for cast metal-work, and there being no demand for casting, there was no practice either in its cognate preliminary art of moulding clay. Hence, such bronze work as originated was very unsatisfactory; the lack of skill in casting, and the consequent elaboration of bronze-work with the file, lasting late into the Renaissance. But the men of the Middle Ages were marvellously skilful carvers of stone. Architecture, ever since the Roman time, had given more and more importance to sculptured ornament: already exquisite in the early Byzantine screens and capitals, it developed through the elaborate mouldings, traceries, and columns of the Lombard style into the art of elaborate reliefs and groups of the full-blown Gothic; indeed the Gothic church is, in Italy, the work no longer of the mason, but of the sculptor. It is no empty coincidence that the hillside villages which still supply Florence with stone and with stonemasons should have given their names to three of its greatest sculptors, Mino da Fiesole, Desiderio da Settignano, and Benedetto da Maiano; that Michelangelo should have told Vasari that the chisel and mallet had come to him with the milk of his nurse, a stonecutter's wife from those same slopes, down which jingle to-day the mules carting ready-shaped stone from the quarries. The mediæval Tuscans, the Pisans of the thirteenth, and the Florentines of the fifteenth century, evidently made small wax or clay sketches of their statues; but their works are conceived and executed in the marble, and their art has come out of the stone without interposition of other material, even as the figures which Michelangelo chopped, living and colossal, direct out of the block.[1]

The Greek, therefore, was a moulder of clay, a caster of bronze, in the early time when the art acquires its character and takes its direction; in that period, on the contrary, the Tuscan was a chaser of silver, a hammerer of iron, above all a cutter of stone. Now clay (and we must remember that bronze is originally clay) means the modelled plane and succession of planes smoothed and rounded by the finger, the imitation of all nature's gently graduated swellings and depressions, the absolute form as it exists to the touch; but clay does not give interesting light and shade, and bronze is positively blurred by high lights; and neither clay nor bronze has any resemblance to the texture of human limbs or drapery: it gives the form, but not the stuff. It is the exact reverse with marble. Granulated like a living fibre, yet susceptible of a delicate polish, it can imitate the actual substance of human flesh, with its alternations of opacity and luminousness; it can reproduce, beneath the varied strokes of the chisel, the grain, running now one way, now another, which is given to the porous skin by the close-packed bone and

[1] Interesting details in Vasari's treatise, and in his Lives of J. della Quercia, Ferrucci, and other sculptors.

muscle below. Moreover, it is so docile, so soft, yet so resistent, that the iron can cut it like butter or engrave it lightly like agate; so that the shadows may pour deep into chasms and pools, or run over the surface in a network of shallow threads; light and shade becoming the artist's material as much as the stone itself.

The Greek, as a result, perceived form not as an appearance, but as a reality; saw with the eye the complexities of projection and depression perceivable by the hand. His craft was that of measurements, of minute proportion, of delicate concave and convex—in one word, of *planes*. His dull, malleable clay, and ductile, shining bronze had taught him nothing of the way in which light and shadow corrode, blur, and pattern a surface. His fancy, his skill, embraced the human form like the gypsum of the moulder, received the stamp of its absolute being. The beauty he sought was concrete, actual, the same in all lights and from all points of view: the comely man himself, not the beautiful marble picture.

The marble picture, on the other hand—a picture in however high and complete relief—a picture for a definite point of view, arranged by receiving light projected at a given angle on a surface cut deep or shallow especially to receive it—was produced by the sculpture that spontaneously grew out of the architectural stone-cutting of the Byzantine and Lombard schools. The mouldings on a church, still more the stone ornaments of its capitals, pulpit, and choir rails, seen, as they are,

K

each at various and peculiar heights above the eye, under light which, however varying, can never get behind or above them if outdoor, below or in flank if indoor—these mouldings, part of a great architectural pattern of black and white, inevitably taught the masons all the subtle play of light and surface, all the deceits of position and perspective. And the mere manipulation of the marble taught them, as we have seen, the exquisite finenesses of surface, texture, crease, accent, and line. What the figure actually was—the real proportions and planes, the actual form of the model—did not matter; no hand was to touch it, no eye to measure; it was to be delightful only in the position which the artist chose, and in no other had it a right to be seen.

II

These were the two arts, originating from a material and a habit of work which were entirely different, and which produced artistic necessities diametrically opposed. It might be curious to speculate upon what would have resulted had their position in history been reversed; what statues we should possess had the marble-carving art born of architectural decoration originated in Greece, and the art of clay and bronze flourished in Christian and mediæval Italy. Be this as it may, the accident of the surroundings—of the habits of life and thought which pressed on the artist, and combined with the necessities of his material method—appears to have intensified the peculiarities organic in each of the two sculptures. I say *appears*, because we must bear in mind that the combination was merely fortuitous, and guard against the habit of thinking that because a type is familiar it is therefore alone conceivable.

We all know all about the antique and the mediæval *milieu*. It is useless to recapitulate the influence, on the one hand, of antique civilisation, with its southern outdoor existence, its high training of the body, its draped citizens, naked athletes, and half-clothed work-folk, its sensuous religion of earthly gods and muscular demigods; or the influence, on the other hand, of the more complex life of the Middle Ages, essentially northern in type, sedentary and manufacturing, huddled in unventilated towns, with its constant pre-occupation, even among the most sordid grossness, of the splendour of the soul, the beauty of suffering, the ignominy of the body, and the dangers of bodily prosperity. Of all this we have heard even too much, thanks to the picturesqueness which has recommended the *milieu* of Monsieur Taine to writers more mindful of literary effect than of the philosophy of art. But there is another historical circumstance whose influence, in differentiating Greek sculpture from the sculpture of mediæval Italy, can scarcely be overrated. It is that, whereas in ancient Greece sculpture was the important, fully developed art, and painting merely its shadow; in mediæval Italy painting was the art which best answered the requirements of the civilisation, the art struggling with the most important problems; and that painting therefore reacted strongly upon sculpture. Greek painting was the shadow of Greek sculpture in an almost literal sense: the figures on wall and base, carefully modelled, without texture, symmetrically arranged alongside of each other regardless of pictorial pattern, seem indeed to be projected on to the flat surface by the statues; they are, most certainly, the shadow of modelled figures cast on the painter's mind.

The sculptor could learn nothing new from paintings where all that is proper to painting is ignored:—plane always preferred to line, the constructive details, perceptible only as projection, not as colour or value (like the insertion of the leg and the thigh), marked by deep lines that look like tattoo marks; and perspective almost entirely ignored, at least till a late period. It is necessary thus to examine Greek painting[1] in order to appreciate, by comparison with this negative art, the very positive influence of mediæval painting or mediæval sculpture. The painting on a flat surface—fresco or panel—which became more and more the chief artistic expression of those times, taught men to consider perspective; and, with perspective and its possibility of figures on many planes, grouping: the pattern that

[1] At all events, Greek painting preceding or contemporaneous with the great period of sculpture. Later painting was, of course, much more pictorial.

must arise from juxtaposed limbs and heads. It taught them to perceive form no longer as projection or plane; but as line and light and shade, as something whose charm lay mainly in the boundary curves, the silhouette, so much more important in one single, unchangeable position than where, the eye wandering round a statue, the only moderate interest of one point of view is compensated by the additional interest of another. Moreover, painting, itself the product of a much greater interest in colour than Antiquity had known, forced upon men's attention the important influence of colour upon form. For, although the human being, if we abstract the element of colour, if we do it over with white paint, has indeed the broad, somewhat vague form, the indecision of lines which characterises antique sculpture; yet the human being as he really exists, with his coloured hair, eyes, and lips, his cheeks, forehead, and chin patterned with tint, has a much greater sharpness, precision, contrast of form, due to the additional emphasis of the colour. Hence, as pictorial perspective and composition undoubtedly inclined sculptors to seek greater complexities of relief and greater unity of point of view, so the new importance of drawing and colouring suggested to them a new view of form. A human being was no longer a mere arrangement of planes and of masses, homogeneous in texture and colour. He was made of different substances, of hair, skin over fat, muscle, or bone, skin smooth, wrinkled, or stubbly, and, besides this, he was painted different colours. He had, moreover, what the Greeks had calmly whitewashed away, or replaced by an immovable jewel or enamel: that extraordinary and extraordinarily various thing called an Eye.

All these differences between the monochrome creature—colour abstracted—of the Greeks and the mottled real human being, the sculptors of the Renaissance were led to perceive by their brothers the painters; and having perceived, they were dissatisfied at having to omit in their representation. But how show that they too had seen them?

Here return to our notice two other peculiarities which distinguish mediæval sculpture from antique: first, that mediæval sculpture, rarely called upon for free open-air figures, was for ever producing architectural ornament, seen at a given height and against a dark background; and indoor decoration seen under an unvarying and often defective light; and secondly, that mediæval sculpture was the handicraft of the subtle carver in delicate stone.

The sculpture which was an essential part of Lombard and Gothic architecture required a treatment that should adapt it to its particular place and subordinate it to a given effect. According to the height above the eye and the direction of the light, certain details had to be exaggerated, certain others suppressed; a sculptured window, like those of Orsanmichele, would not give the delightful pattern of black and white unless some surfaces were more raised than others, some portions of figure or leafage allowed to sink into quiescence, others to start forward by means of the black rim of undercutting; and a sepulchral monument, raised thirty feet above the spectator's eye, like those inside Sta. Maria Novella, would present a mere intricate confusion unless the recumbent figure, the canopy, and various accessories, were such as to seem unnatural at the level of the eye. Thus, the heraldic lions of one of these Gothic tombs have the black cavity of the jaw cut by marble bars which are absolutely out of proportion to the rest of the creature's body, and to the detail of the other features, but render the showing of the teeth even at the other side of the transept. Again, in the more developed art of the fifteenth century, Rossellino's Cardinal of Portugal has the offside of his face shelved upwards so as to catch the light, because he is seen from below, and the near side would otherwise be too prominent; while the beautiful dead warrior, by an unknown sculptor, at Ravenna has had a portion of his jaw and chin deliberately cut away, because the spectator is intended to look down upon his recumbent figure. If we take a cast of the Cardinal's head and look down upon it, or hang a cast of the dead warrior on the wall, the whole appearance alters; the expression is almost reversed and the features are distorted. On the other hand, a cast from a real head, placed on high like the Cardinal's, would become insignificant, and laid at the height of a table, like the dead warrior's, would look lumbering and tumid. Thus, again, the head of Donatello's Poggio, which is visible and intelligible placed high up in the darkness of the Cathedral of Florence, looks as if it had been gashed and hacked with a blunt knife when seen in the cast at the usual height in an ordinary light.

Now this subtle circumventing of distance, height, and darkness; this victory of pattern over place; this reducing of light and shadow into tools for the sculptor, mean, as we see from the above examples, sacrificing the reality to the appearance, altering the proportions and planes so rigorously reproduced by the Greeks, mean sacrificing the sacred absolute form. And such a habit of taking liberties with what can be measured by the hand, in order to please the eye, allowed the sculptors of the Renaissance to think of their model no longer as the homogeneous *white man* of the Greeks, but as a creature in whom structure was accentuated, intensified, or contradicted by colour and texture.

Furthermore, these men of the fifteenth century possessed the cunning carving which could make stone vary in texture, in fibre, and almost in colour.

A great many biographical details substantiate the evidence of statues and busts that the sculptors of the Renaissance carried on their business in a different manner from the ancient Greeks. The great development in Antiquity of the art of casting bronze, carried on everywhere for the production of weapons and household furniture, must have accustomed Greek sculptors (if we may call them by that name) to limit their personal work to the figure modelled in clay. And the great number of their works, many tediously constructed of ivory and gold, shows clearly that they did not abandon this habit in case of marble statuary, but merely gave the finishing strokes to a copy of their clay model, produced by workmen whose skill must have been fostered by the apparently thriving trade in marble copies of bronzes.

It was different in the Renaissance. Vasari recommends, as obviating certain miscalculations which frequently happened, that sculptors should prepare large models by which to measure the capacities of their block of marble. But these models, described as made of a mixture of plaster, size, and cloth shavings over tow and hay, could serve only for the rough proportions and attitude; nor is there ever any allusion to any process of minute measurement, such as pointing, by which detail could be transferred from the model to the stone. Most often we hear of small wax models which the sculptors enlarged directly in the stone. Vasari, while exaggerating the skill of Michelangelo in making his David out of a block mangled by another sculptor, expresses no surprise at his having chopped the marble himself; indeed, the anecdote itself affords evidence of the commonness of such a practice, since Agostino di Duccio would not have spoilt the block if he had not cut into it rashly without previous comparison with a model.[1] We hear, besides, that Jacopo della Quercia spent twelve years over one of the gates of S. Petronio, and that other sculptors carried out similar great works with the assistance of one man, or with no assistance at all,—a proceeding which would have seemed the most frightful waste except in a time and country where half of the sculptors were originally stone-masons and the other half goldsmiths, that is to say, men accustomed to every stage, coarse or subtle, of their work. The absence of replicas of Renaissance sculpture, so striking a contrast to the scores of repetitions of Greek works, proves, moreover, that the actual execution in marble was considered an intrinsic part of the sculpture of the fifteenth century, in the same way as the painting of a Venetian master. Phidias might leave the carving of his statues to skilful workmen, once he had modelled the clay, even as the painters of the merely designing and linear schools, Perugino, Ghirlandaio, or Botticelli, might employ pupils to carry out their designs on panel or wall. But in the same way as a Titian is not a Titian without a certain handling of the brush, so a Donatello is not a Donatello, or a Mino not a Mino, without a certain individual excellence in the cutting of the marble.

[1] Several Greek vases and coins show the sculptor modelling his figure; while in Renaissance designs, from that of Nanni di Banco to a mediocre allegorical engraving in an early edition of Vasari, the sculptor, or the personified art of Sculpture, is actually working with chisel and mallet.

These men brought, therefore, to the cutting of marble a degree of skill and knowledge of which the ancients had no notion, as they had no necessity. In their hands the chisel was not merely a second modelling tool, moulding delicate planes, uniting insensibly broad masses of projection and depression. It was a pencil, which, according as it was held, could emphasise the forms in sharp hatchings or let them die away unnoticed in subdued, imperceptible washes. It was a brush which could give the texture and the values of the colour—a brush dipped in various tints of light and darkness, according as it poured into the marble the light and the shade, and as it translated into polishings and rough hewings and granulations and every variety of cutting, the texture of flesh, of hair, and of drapery; of the blonde hair and flesh of children, the coarse flesh and bristly hair of old men, the draperies of wool, of linen, and of brocade. The sculptors of Antiquity took a beautiful human being—a youth in his perfect flower, with limbs trained by harmonious exercise and ripened by exposure to the air and sun—and, correcting whatever was imperfect in his individual forms by their hourly experience of similar beauty, they copied in clay as much as clay could give of his perfections: the subtle proportions, the majestic ampleness of masses, the delicate finish of limbs, the harmonious play of muscles, the serene simplicity of look and gesture, placing him in an attitude intelligible and graceful from the greatest possible distance and from the largest variety of points of view. And they preserved this perfect piece of loveliness by handing it over to the faithful copyist in marble, to the bronze, which, more faithful still, fills every minutest cavity left by the clay. Being beautiful in himself, in all his proportions and details, this man of bronze or marble was beautiful wherever he was placed and from wheresoever he was seen; whether he appeared foreshortened on a temple front, or face to face among the laurel trees, whether shaded by a portico, or shining in the blaze of the open street. His beauty must be judged and loved as we should judge and love the beauty of a real human being, for he is the closest reproduction that art has given of beautiful reality placed in reality's real surroundings. He is the embodiment of the strength and purity of youth, untroubled by the moment, independent of place and of circumstance.

Of such perfection, born of the rarest meeting of happy circumstances, Renaissance sculpture knows nothing. A lesser art, for painting was then what sculpture had been in Antiquity; bound more or less closely to the service of architecture; surrounded by ill-grown, untrained bodies; distracted by ascetic feelings and scientific curiosities, the sculpture of Donatello and Mino, of Jacopo della Quercia and Desidirio da Settignano, of Michelangelo himself, was one of those second artistic growths which use up the elements that have been neglected or rejected by the more fortunate and vigorous efflorescence which has preceded. It failed in everything in which antique sculpture had succeeded; it accomplished what Antiquity had left undone. Its sense of bodily beauty was rudimentary; its knowledge of the nude alternately insufficient and pedantic; the forms of Donatello's David and of Benedetto's St. John are clumsy, stunted, and inharmonious; even Michelangelo's Bacchus is but a comely lout. This sculpture has, moreover, a marvellous preference for ugly old men —gross, or ascetically imbecile; and for ill-grown striplings: except the St. George of Donatello, whose body, however, is entirely encased in inflexible leather and steel, it never gives us the perfection and pride of youth. These things are obvious, and set us against the art as a whole. But see it when it does what Antiquity never attempted; Antiquity which placed statues side by side in a gable, balancing one another, but not welded into one pattern; which made relief the mere repetition of one point of view of the round figure, the shadow of the gable group; which, until its decline, knew nothing of the pathos of old age, of the grotesque exquisiteness of infancy, of the endearing awkwardness of adolescence; which knew nothing of the texture of the skin, the silkiness of the hair, the colour of the eye.

III

Let us see Renaissance sculpture in its real achievement.

Here are a number of children by various sculptors

of the fifteenth century. This is the tiny baby whose little feet still project from a sort of gaiter of flesh, whose little boneless legs cannot carry the fat little paunch, the heavy big head. Note that its little skull is still soft, like an apple, under the thin floss hair. Its elder brother or sister is still vaguely contemplative of the world, with eyes that easily grow sleepy in their blueness. Those a little older have learned already that the world is full of solemn people on whom to practise tricks; their features have scarcely accentuated, their hair has merely curled into loose rings, but their eyes have come forward from below the forehead, eyes and forehead working together already; and there are great holes, into which you may dig your thumb, in the cheeks. Those of fourteen or fifteen have deplorably thin arms, and still such terrible calves; and a stomach telling of childish gigantic meals; but they have the pert, humorous frankness of Verrocchio's David, who certainly flung a jest at Goliath's unwieldy person together with his stone; or the delicate, sentimental pretty woman's grace of Donatello's St. John of the Louvre, and Benedetto da Maiano's: they will soon be poring over the *Vita Nuova* and Petrarch. Two other St. Johns—I am speaking of Donatello's—have turned out differently. One, the first beard still doubtful round his mouth, has already rushed madly away from earthly loves; his limbs are utterly wasted by fasting; except his legs, which have become incredibly muscular from continual walking; he has begun to be troubled by voices in the wilderness—whether of angels or of demons—and he flies along, his eyes fixed on his scroll, and with them fixing his mind on unearthly things; he will very likely go mad, this tempted saint of twenty-one. Here he is again, beard and hair matted, almost a wild man of the woods, but with the gravity and self-possession of a preacher; he has come out of the wilderness, overcome all temptations, his fanaticism is now militant and conquering. This is certainly not the same man, but perhaps one of his listeners, this old King David of Donatello—a man at no time intelligent, whose dome-shaped head has taken back, with the thin white floss hair that recalls infancy, an infantine lack of solidity; whose mouth is drooping already, perhaps after a first experience of paralysis, and his eyes getting vague in look; but who, in this intellectual and physical decay, seems to have become only the more full of gentleness and sweetness; misnamed David, a Job become reconciled to his fate by becoming indifferent to himself, an Ancient Mariner who has seen the water-snakes and blessed them and been filled with blessing.

These are all statues or busts intended for a given niche or bracket, a given portico or window, but in a measure free sculpture. Let us now look at what is already decoration. Donatello's Annunciation, the big coarse relief in friable grey stone (incapable of a sharp line), picked out with delicate gilding; no fluttering or fainting, the angel and the Virgin grave, decorous, like the neighbouring pilasters. Again, his organ-loft of flat relief, with granulated groundwork: the flattened groups of dancing children making, with deep, wide shadows beneath their upraised, linked arms, a sort of human trellis-work of black and white. Mino's Madonna at Fiesole: the relief turned and cut so as to look out of the chapel into the church, so that the Virgin's head, receiving the light like a glory on the pure, polished forehead, casts a nimbus of shadow round itself, while the saints are sucked into the background, their accessories only, staff and gridiron, allowed to assert themselves by a sharp shadow; a marvellous vision of white heavenly roses, their pointed buds and sharp spines flourishing on martyrs' blood and incense, grown into the close lips and long eyes, the virginal body and thin hands of Mary. From these reliefs we come to the compositions, group inside group, all shelving into portico and forest vista, of the pulpit of Sta. Croce, the perspective bevelling it into concavities, like those of panelling; the heads and projecting shoulders lightly marked as some carved knob or ornament; to the magnificent compositions in light and shade, all balancing and harmonising each other, and framed round by garlands of immortal blossom and fruit, of Ghiberti's gates.

Nor is this all. The sculpture of the Renaissance, not satisfied with having portrayed the real human being made of flesh and blood, of bone and skin, dark-eyed or flaxen-haired, embodied in the marble the impalpable forms of dreams. Its latest, greatest, works are those sepulchres of Michelangelo, whose pinnacle enthrones strange ghosts of warriors, and whose steep sides are the unquiet couch of divinities hewn, you would say, out of darkness and the light that is as darkness.

A SEEKER OF PAGAN PERFECTION

A SEEKER OF PAGAN PERFECTION

BEING THE LIFE OF DOMENICO NERONI,
PICTOR SACRILEGUS

EVERY time, of late years, of my being once more in Rome, I have been subject to a peculiar mental obsession: retracing my steps, if not materially, in fancy at least, to such parts of the city as bear witness to the strange meeting of centuries, where the Middle Ages have altered to their purposes, or filled with their significance, the ruined remains of Antiquity.

Such places are scarcer than one might have expected, and for that reason perhaps more impressive, more fragmentary and enigmatic. There are the colossal columns—great trickles and flakes of black etching as with acid their marble—of the temple of Mars Ultor, with that Tuscan palace of Torre della Milizia rising from among them. There is, inside Ara Cœli—itself commemorating the legend of Augustus and the Sibyl—the tomb of Dominus Pandulphus Sabelli, its borrowed vine-garlands and satyrs and Cupids surmounted by mosaic crosses and Gothic inscriptions; and outside the same church, on a ground of green and gold, a Mother of God looking down from among gurgoyles and escutcheons on to the marble river-god of the yard of the Capitol below. Then also, where pines and laurels still root in the unrifled tombs, the skeleton feudal fortress, gutted as by an earthquake, alongside of the tower of Cæcilia Metella. These were the places to which my thoughts were for ever recurring; to them, and to nameless other spots, the street-corner, for instance, where an Ionic pillar, with beaded and full-horned capital, is walled into the side of an insignificant modern house. I know not whether, in consequence of this straining to see the meeting-point of Antiquity and the Middle Ages (like the fancy, sometimes experienced, to reach the confluence of rivers), or rather as a cause thereof, but a certain story has long lurked in the corners of my mind. Twenty years have passed since first I was aware of its presence, and it has undergone many changes. It is presumably a piece of my inventing, for I have neither read it nor heard it related. But by this time it has acquired a certain traditional veracity in my eyes, and I give to the reader rather as historical fact than as fiction the study which I have always called to myself: *Pictor Sacrilegus.*

I

Domenico, the son of Luca Neroni, painter, sculptor, goldsmith, and engraver, about whom, owing either to the scarcity of his works or the scandal of his end, Vasari has but a few words in another man's biography, must have been born shortly before or shortly after the year 1450, a contemporary of Perugino, of Ghirlandaio, of Filippino Lippi, and of Signorelli, by all of whom he was influenced at various moments, and whom he influenced by turns.

He was born and bred in the Etruscan town of Volterra, of a family which for generations had exercised the art of the goldsmith, stimulated, perhaps, by the sight of ornaments discovered in Etruscan tombs, and carrying on, peradventure, some of the Etruscan traditions of two thousand years before. The mountain city, situate on the verge of the malarious seaboard of Southern Tuscany, is reached from one side through windings of barren valleys, where the dried-up brooks are fringed, instead of reed, with the grey, sand-loving tamarisk; and from the other side, across a high-lying moorland of stunted heather and sere grass, whence the larks rise up scared by only a flock of sheep or a mare and her foal, and you journey for miles without meeting a house or a clump of cypresses. In front, with the white road zigzagging along their crests, is a wilderness of barren, livid hillocks, separated by huge fissures and crevassed by huge cracks, with here and there separate rocks, projecting like Druidic stones from the valley of gaping ravines; and beyond them all a higher mountain, among whose rocks and ilexes you doubtfully distinguish the walls and towers of the Etruscan city. A mass of Cyclopean wall and great black houses, grim with stone brackets and iron hooks and stanchions, all for defence and barricade, Volterra looks down into the deep valleys, like the vague heraldic animal, black and bristly, which peers from the high tower of the municipal palace. One wonders how this could ever have been a city of the fat, voluptuous Etruscans, whose images lie propped up and wide-eyed on their stone coffin-lids. The long wars of old Italic times, in which Etruria fell before Rome, must have burned and destroyed, as one would think, the land as well as the inhabitants, leaving but grey cinders and blackened stone behind. Siena and Florence ruined Volterra once more in the Middle Ages, isolating it near the pestilential Maremma and checking its growth outward and inward. The cathedral, the pride of a mediæval commonwealth, is still a mean and unfinished building of the twelfth century. There is no native art, of any importance, of a later period; what the town possesses has come from other parts, the altar-pieces by Matteo di Giovanni and Signorelli, for instance, and the marble candelabra, carried by angels, of the school of Mino da Fiesole.

In this remote and stagnant town, the artistic training of Domenico Neroni was necessarily imperfect and limited throughout his boyhood to the paternal goldsmith's craft. Indeed, it seems likely that some peculiarities of his subsequent life as an artist, his laboriousness disproportionate to all results, his persistent harping on unimportant detail, and his exclusive interest in line and curve, were due not merely to an unhappy and laborious temperament, but also to the long habit of an art full of manual skill and cunning tradition, which presented the eye with ingenious patterns, but rarely attempted, save in a few church ornaments, more of the domain of sculpture, to tell a story or express a feeling.

Besides this influence of his original trade, we find in Domenico Neroni's work the influence of his early surroundings. His native country is such as must delight, or help to form, a painter of pale anatomies. The painters of Southern Tuscany loved as a background the arid and mountainous country of their birth. Taddeo di Bartolo placed the Death of the Virgin among the curious undulations of pale clay and sandy marl that stretch to the southernmost gates of Siena; Signorelli was amused and fascinated by the odd cliffs and overhanging crags, unnatural and grotesque like some Druidic monument, of the valleys of the Paglia and the Chiana; and Pier della Francesca has left, in the allegorical triumphs of Frederick of Urbino and his duchess, studies most exquisite and correct, of what meets the traveller's eyes on the watersheds of the central Apennine, sharp-toothed lines of mountain peaks pale against the sky, dim distant whiteness of sea, and valleys and roads and torrents twisting intricately as on a map. The country about Volterra, revealing itself with rosy lividness at dawn, with delicate periwinkle blue at sunset, through an open city gate or a gap between the tall black houses, helped to make Neroni a lover of muscle and sinew, of the strength and suppleness of movement, of the osseous structure divined within the limbs; and made him shrink all his life long, not merely from drapery or costume that blunted the lines of the body, but from any warmth and depth of colour; till the figures stood out like ghosts, or people in faded tapestries, from the pale lilacs and greys and washed out cinnamons of his backgrounds. For the bold peaks and swelling mountains of the valleys of the Arno and the Tiber, and the depths of colour among vegetation and rivers, seemed crude and emphatic to a man who carried in his memory those bosses of hill, pearly where the waters have washed the sides, pale golden buff where a little sere grass covers the rounded top; those great cracks and chasms, with the white road snaking along the narrow table-land and the wide valleys; and the ripple of far-off mountain chains, strong and restrained in curves, exquisite in tints, like the dry white and purpled hemlock, and the dusty lilac scabius, which seem to flower alone in that arid and melancholy and beautiful country.

"Colour," wrote Domenico Neroni, among a mass of notes on his art, measurements, and calculations, "is the enemy of noble art. It is the enemy of all precise and perfect form, since where colour exists form can be seen only as juxtaposition of colour. For this reason it has pleased the Creator to lend colour only to the inanimate world, as to senseless vegetables and plants, and to the lower kinds of living creatures, as birds, fishes, and reptiles; whereas nobler creatures, as lions, tigers, horses, cattle, stags, and unicorns, are robed in white or dull skins, the noblest breeds, indeed, both of horses, as those of the Soldans of Egypt and Numidia, and of oxen, as those of the valleys of the Clitumnus and Chiana, being white; whence, indeed, the poet Virgil has said that such latter are fittest for sacrifice to the immortal gods; 'hinc albi, Clitumne, greges,' and what follows. And man, the masterpiece of creation, is white; and only in the less noble portions of his body, which have no sensitiveness and no shape (being, indeed, vegetative and deciduous), as hair and beard, partaking of colour. Wherefore the ancient Romans and Greeks, portraying their gods, chose white marble for material, and not gaudy porphyry or jasper, and portrayed them naked. Whence certain moderns, calling themselves painters, who muffle our Lord and the Holy Apostles in many-coloured garments, thinking thereby to do a seemly and honourable thing, but really proceeding basely like tailors, might take a lesson if they could."

The quotation from Virgil, and the allusion to the statues of the immortal gods, shows that Neroni must have written these lines in the later part of his career, when already under the influence of that humanist Filarete, who played so important a part in his life, and when possessed already by those notions which brought him to so strange and fearful an end. But from his earliest years he sought for form, despising other things. He passed with contempt through a six months' apprenticeship at Perugia, railing at the great factory of devotional art established there by Perugino, of whom, with his rows of splay-footed saints and spindle-shanked heroes, he spoke with the same sweeping contempt as later Michelangelo. At Siena, which he described (much as its earlier artists painted it) as a town of pink toy-houses and scarlet toy-towers, he found nothing to admire save the marble fountain of Jacopo della Quercia, for the antique group of the Three Graces, later to be drawn by the young Raphael, had not yet been given to the cathedral by the nephew of Pius II. The sight of these noble reliefs, particularly of the one representing Adam and Eve driven out of Paradise, with their strong and well-understood nudities, determined him to exchange painting for sculpture, and made him hasten to Florence to see the works of Donatello and of Ghiberti.

Domenico Neroni must have spent several years of his life—between 1470 and 1480—in Florence, but little of his work has remained in that city,—little, at least, that we can identify with certainty. For taking service, as he did, with the Pollaiolos, Verrocchio, Nanni di Banco, and even with Filippino and Botticelli, wherever his inquisitive mind could learn, or his restless, fastidious, laborious talent gain him bread, it is presumable that much of his work might be discovered alongside that of his masters, in the collective productions of the various workshops. It is possible thus that he had a hand in much metal and relief work of the Pollaiolos, and perhaps even in the embroidering and tapestries of which they were undertakers; also in certain ornaments, friezes of Cupids and dolphins, and exquisite shell and acanthus carving of the monuments of Santa Croce; and it may be surmised that he occasionally assisted Botticelli in his perspective and anatomy, since that master took him to Rome when commissioned to paint in the chapel of Pope Sixtus. Indeed, in certain little-known studies for Botticelli's Birth of Venus and Calumny of Apelles one may discover, in the strong sweep of the outline, in the solid fashion in which the figures are planted on their feet—all peculiarities which disappear in the painted pictures, where grace of motion and exquisitive research take the place of solid draughtsmanship—the hand of the artist whom the restless desire to confront ever new problems alone prevented from attaining a place among the great men of his time.

For there was in Domenico Neroni, from the very outset of his career, a curiosity after the hidden, a passion for the unattainable, which kept him, with greater power than many of his contemporaries, and vastly greater science, a mere student throughout his lifetime. He resembled in some respects his great contemporary Leonardo, but while the eager inquisitiveness of the latter was tempered by a singular power of universal enjoyment, a love of luxury and joyousness in every form, the intellectual activity of Neroni was exasperated into a kind of unhappy mania by the fact that its satisfaction was the only happiness that he could conceive. He would never have understood, or understanding would have detested, the luxurious *dilettante* spirit which made Leonardo prefer painting to sculpture, because whereas the sculptor is covered with a mud of marble dust, and works in a place disorderly with chips and rubbish, the painter "sits at his easel, well dressed and at ease, in a clean house adorned with pictures, his work accompanied by music or the reading of delightful books, which, untroubled by the sound of hammering and other noises, may be listened to with very great pleasure." The workshop of Neroni, when he had one of his own, was full of cobwebs and dust, littered with the remains of frugal and unsavoury meals, and resolutely closed to the rich and noble persons in whose company Leonardo delighted. And if Neroni, in his many-sided activity, eventually put aside sculpture for painting, it was merely because, as he was wont to say, a figure must needs look real when it is solid and you can walk round it; but to make men and women rise out of a flat canvas or plastered wall, and stand and move as if alive, is truly the work of a god.

Men and women, said Neroni; and he should have added men and women nude. For the studies which he made of the anatomy of horses and dogs were destined merely to shed light on the construction of human creatures; and his elaborate and exquisite drawings of undulating hills and sinuous rivers, nay, of growths of myrtle and clumps of daffodils, were intended as practice towards drawing the more subtle lines and curves of man's body. And as to clothes, he could not understand that great anatomists like Signorelli should huddle their figures quite willingly in immense cloaks and gowns; still less how exquisite draughtsmen like his friend Botticelli (who had the sense of line like no other man since Frate Lippo, although his people were oddly out of joint) could take pleasure in putting half-a-dozen veils atop of each other, and then tying them all into bunches and bunches with innumerable bits of tape! As to himself, he invariably worked out every detail of the nude, in the vain hope that the priests and monks for whom he worked would allow at least half of those beautiful anatomies to remain visible; and when, with infinite difficulties and bad language, he gradually gave in to the necessity of some sort of raiment, it was of such a nature—the hose and jerkins of the men-at-arms like a second skin, the draperies of the womankind as clinging as if they had been picked out of the river, that a great many pious people absolutely declined to pay the agreed on sum for paintings more suited to Pagan than to Christian countries; and indeed Fra Girolamo Savonarola included much work of Domenico's in his very finest burnings.

Such familiarity with nude form was not easily attained in the fifteenth century. Mediæval civilisation gave no opportunities for seeing naked or half-naked people moving freely as in the antique palæstra; and there had yet been discovered too few antique marbles for the empiric knowledge of ancient sculptors to be empirically inherited by modern ones. Observation of the hired model, utterly insufficient in itself, required to be supplemented by a thorough science of the body's mechanism. But physiology and surgery were still in their infancy; and artists could not, as they could after the teachings of Vesalius, Fallopius, and Cesalpinus, avail themselves of the science accumulated for medical purposes. Verrocchio and the Pollaiolos most certainly, and Donatello almost without a doubt, practised dissection as a part of their business, as Michelangelo, with the advantage of twenty years of their researches behind him, practised it passionately in his turn. Of all the men of his day, Domenico Neroni, however, was the most fervent anatomist. He ran every risk of contagion and of punishment in order to procure corpses from the hospital and the gibbet. He undermined his constitution by breathing and handling corruption, and when his friends implored him to spare his health, he would answer, although unable to touch food for sickness, by paraphrasing the famous words of Paolo Uccello, and exclaiming from among his grisly and abominable properties, "Ah! how sweet a thing is not anatomy!"

There was nothing, he said—for he spoke willingly to any one who questioned him on these subjects—

more beautiful than the manner in which human beings are built, or indeed living creatures of any kind; for, in the scarcity of corpses and skeletons, he would pick up on his walks the bones of sheep that had died on the hill-sides, or those of horses and mules furbished up by the scavenger dogs of the river-edge. It was marvellous to listen to him when he was in the vein. He sat handling horrible remains and talking about them like a lover about his mistress or a preacher about God; indeed, bones, muscles, and tendons were mistress and god all in one to this fanatical lover of human form. He would insist on the loveliness of line of the scapula, finding in the sweep of the *acromion* ridge a fanciful resemblance to the pinion, and in the angular shape of the *coracoid* process to the neck and head of a raven in full flight. Following with his finger the triangular outline of the bone, he went on to explain how its freedom of movement is due to its singular independence; laid loosely on the flat muscles behind the upper ribs, it moves with absolute freedom, backwards and forwards, up and down, unconnected with any other bone, till, turning the corner of the shoulder, it is hinged rather than tied to the collar-bone; the collar-bone itself free to move upwards from its articulation in the sternum. And then talk of the great works of man! Talk of Brunellesco and his cupola, of the engineers of the Duke of Calabria! Look at the human arm: what engineer would have dared to fasten anything to such a movable base as that? Yet an arm can swing round

M

like a windmill, and lift weights like the stoutest crane without being wrenched out of its sockets, because the muscles act as pulleys in four different directions. And see, under the big *deltoid*, which fits round the shoulder like an epaulette and pulls the arm up, is the scapular group, things like tidily sorted skeins, thick on the shoulder-blades, diminished to a tendon string at their insertion in the arm; their business is to pull the arm back, in opposition to the big pectoral muscle which pulls it forwards. Here you have your arm working up, backwards or forwards; but how about pulling it down? An exquisite little arrangement settles that. Instead of being inserted with the rest on the outside of the arm-bone, the lowest muscle takes another road, and is inserted in the under part of the bone, in company with the great *latissimus dorsi*, and these tightening while the *deltoid* slackens, pull the arm down. No other arrangement could have done it with so little bulk; and an additional muscle on the under-arm or the ribs would have spoilt the figure of Apollo himself.

Among the paintings of contemporary artists, the one which at that time afforded Domenico the most unmingled satisfaction was Pollaiolo's tiny panel of Hercules and the Hydra. There! You might cover it with the palm of your hand; but in that hand you would be holding the concentrated strength and valour of the world, the true son of Jove, the most beautiful muscles that ever were seen! At least the most beautiful save in the statues of Donatello; for, of course, Donato was the greatest craftsman that had ever lived; and Domenico spoke of him as, in Vasari's day, men were to speak of Michelangelo.

For I ask you, who save an angel in human shape could have modelled that David, so young and triumphant and modest, treading on Goliath's head, with toes just slightly turned downwards, and those sandals, of truly divine workmanship? And that St. John in the Wilderness—how beautiful are not his ribs, showing under the wasted pectoral muscles; and how one sees that the *radius* rolls across the *ulna* in the forearm; surely one's heart, rather than the statue, must be made of stone if one can contemplate without rapture the exquisite rendering of the texture where the shinbone stands out from the muscles of the leg. Such must have been the works of those famous Romans and Greeks, Phidias and Praxiteles.

Such were the notions of Domenico of Volterra in the earlier part of his career. For a change came gradually upon him after his first visit to Rome, whither, about 1480, he accompanied Botticelli, Rosselli, and Ghirlandaio, whom His Beatitude Pope Sixtus had sent for to decorate the new chapel of the palace.

II

We must not be deluded, like Domenico Neroni during his Florentine days, into the easy mistake of considering mere realism as the veritable aim of the art of his days. Deep in the life of that art, and struggling for ever through whatever passion for scientific accuracy, technical skill, or pathetic expression, is the sense of line and proportion, the desire for pattern, growing steadily till its triumph under Michelangelo and Raphael.

This reveals itself earliest in architecture. The men of the fifteenth century had lost all sense of the logic of construction. Columns, architraves, friezes, and the various categories of actual stone and brick work, occurred to them merely as so much line and curve, applicable to the surface of their buildings, with not more reference to their architecture than a fresco or an arras. The Pazzi Chapel, for instance, is one agglomeration of architectural members which perform no architectural function; but, taken as a piece of surface decoration, say as a stencilling, what could be more harmonious? Or take Alberti's famous church at Rimini; it is but a great piece of architectural veneering, nothing that meets the eye doing any real constructive duty, its exquisite decoration no more closely connected with the building than the strips of damask and yards of gold braid used in other places on holidays. As the fifteenth century treats the architectural detail of Græco-Roman art, so likewise does it proceed with its sculptured ornament; all meaning vanishes before the absorbing interest in pattern. For there is in antique architectural ornament a much larger proportion of significance than can strike us at first. Thus the garlands of ivy and fruit had actually hung round the tomb before being carved on its sides; before ornamenting its corners the rams' heads and skulls of oxen had lain for centuries on the altar. The medallions of nymphs, centaurs, tritons, which to us are so meaningless and irrelevant, had a reference either to the divinity or to the worshippers; and there is probably almost as much spontaneous symbolism in the little cinerary box in the Capitol (of a person called Felix), with its variously employed genii, making music, carrying lanterns and torches, burning or extinguished under a trellis hung with tragic masks, as in any Gothic tomb with angels drawing the curtains of the deathbed. There has been, with the change of religion, an interruption in the symbolic tradition; yet, though we no longer interpret with readiness this dead language of paganism, we feel, if we are the least attentive, that it contains a real meaning. We feel that the sculptors cared not merely for the representation, but also for the object represented. These things were dear to them, a part of their life, their worship, their love; and they put as much observation into their work as any Gothic sculptor, and often as much fancy and humour (though both more beautiful), as one may judge, with plenty of comparison at hand, by a certain antique altar in Siena Cathedral, none of whose Gothic animals come up to the wonderful half-human rams' heads and bored, cross griffins of this forlorn fragment of paganism. The significance of classic ornament the men of the fifteenth century straightway overlooked. They laid hold of it as merely so much form, joining sirens, griffins, garlands, rams' heads, victories, without a suspicion that they might mean or suggest anything. They do, in fact, mean nothing, in most Florentine work, besides exquisite pattern; in the less subtle atmosphere of Venice they reach that frank senselessness which has moved the wrath of Ruskin. But what a charm have not even those foolish monuments of doges and admirals, tier upon tier of triumphal arch, of delicately flowered column and scalloped niche, and then rows of dainty warriors and virtues; how full of meaning to the eye and spirit is not this art so meaningless to the literary mind!

Of course the painting of that age never became an art of mere pattern like the architecture. The whole life and thought of the time was poured into it; and the art itself developed in its upward movement a number of scientific interests—perspective, anatomy, expression—which counteracted that tendency to seek for mere beauty of arrangement and detail. Yet the perfection of Renaissance art never lies in any realism in our modern sense, still less in such suggestiveness as belongs to our literary age; and its triumph is when Raphael can vary and co-ordinate the greatest number of heads, of hands, feet, and groups, as in the School of Athens, the Parnassus, the marvellous little Bible histories of the Loggie; above all, in that "Vision of Ezekiel," which is the very triumph of compact and harmonious composition; when Michelangelo can tie human beings into the finest knots, twist them into the most shapely brackets, frameworks, and key-stones. Even throughout the period of utmost realism, while art was struggling with absorbing problems, men never dreamed of such realism as ours. They never painted a corner of nature at random, merely for the sake of veracity; they never modelled a modern man or woman in their real everyday dress and at their real everyday business. In the midst of everything composition ruled supreme, and each object must needs find its echo, be worked into a scheme of lines, or, with the Venetians, of symmetrically arranged colours. There is an anatomical engraving by Antonio Pollaiolo, one of the strongest realists of his time, which sums up the tendencies of fifteenth-century art. It is a combat of twelve naked men, extraordinarily hideous and in hideous attitudes, but they are so arranged that their ungainly and flayed-looking limbs form with the background of gigantic ivy tendrils an intricate and beautiful pattern, such as we find in Morris's paper and stuffs.

This hankering after pattern, this desire for beauty as such, became manifest in Domenico Neroni after his first sojourn in Rome.

The Roman basilicas, with their stately rows of columns, Corinthian and Ionic, taken from some former temple, and their sunken floor, solemn with Byzantine patterns of porphyry and serpentine, had impressed with their simplicity and harmony the mind of this

Florentine, surrounded hitherto by the intricacies of Gothic buildings. They had formed the link to those fragments of ancient architecture, more intact but also more hidden than in our days, whose dignity of proportion and grace of detail—vast rosetted arches and slender rows of fluted pillars—our modern and Hellenicised taste has treated with too ready contempt. For this Vitruvian art, unoriginal and bungling in the eyes of our purists, was yet full of the serenity, the ampleness which the Middle Ages lacked, and affected the men of the fifteenth century much like a passage of Virgil after a canto of Dante. It formed the fit setting for those remains of antique sculpture which were then gradually beginning to be drawn from the earth. Of such statues and reliefs—which the men of the Renaissance regarded as the work rather of ancient Rome than of Greece—a certain amount was beginning to be carried all over Italy, and notably to the houses of the rich Florentine merchants, who incrusted their staircase walls with inscriptions and carvings, and set statues and sarcophagi under the columns of their courtyards. But such sculpture was chosen rather for its portable character than its excellence; and although single busts and slabs were diligently studied by Florentine artists, there could not have existed in Florence a number of antiques sufficient to impress the ideal of ancient art upon men surrounded on all sides by the works of mediæval painters and sculptors.

To the various sights of Rome must be due that

sudden enlarging of style, that kind of new classicism, which distinguishes the work of fifteenth-century masters after their visit to the Eternal City, enabling Ghirlandaio, Signorelli, Perugino, and Botticelli to make the Sixtine Chapel, and even the finical Pinturicchio, the Vatican library, into centres of fresh influence for harmony and beauty.

The result upon Domenico Neroni was a momentary confusion in all his artistic conceptions. Too much of a seeker for new things, for secret and complicated knowledge, to undergo a mere widening of style like his more gifted or more placid contemporaries, he fell foul of his previous work and his previous masters, without finding a new line or new ideals. The frescoes of Castagno, the little panels of the Pollaiolos, nay, even the works of Donatello, were no longer what they had seemed before his Roman journey, and even what he had remembered them in Rome; for it is with more noble things, even as with the rooms which we inhabit, which strike us as small and dingy only on returning from larger and better lighted ones.

It is to this period of incipient but ill-understood classicism that belongs the only work of Domenico Neroni—at least the only work still extant nowadays—which possesses, over and above its artistic or scientific merit, that indefinable quality which we must simply call *charm;* to this time, with the one exception of the famous woodcuts done for Filarete. Domenico began about this time, and probably under the stress of necessity, to make frontispieces for the books with which Florentine printers were rapidly superseding the manuscripts of twenty years before : collections of sermons, of sonnets, lives of saints, editions of Virgil and Terence, quaint versified encyclopædias, and even books on medicine and astrology. From these little woodcuts, groups of saints round the Cross, with Giotto's tower and Brunellesco's dome in the distance, pictures of Fathers of the Church or ancient poets seated at desks in neatly panelled closets—always with their globes, books, and pot of lilies, and a vista of cloisters; or battles between chaste viragos, in flying Botticellian draperies, and slim, naked Cupids; from such frontispieces Domenico passed on to larger woodcuts, destined to illustrate books never printed, or perhaps, like the so-called *playing cards of Mantegna* and certain prints of Robetta, to be bought as cheap ornaments for walls. Some of those that remain to us have a classical stiffness, reminding one of the Paduan school; others, and these his best, remind one of the work of Botticelli. There is, for instance, the figure of a Muse, elaborately modelled under her ample drapery, seated cross-legged by a playing fountain, on a carpet of exquisitely designed ground-ivy, a little bare trellis behind her, a tortoise lyre in her hand; which has in it somewhat of that odd, vague, questioning character, half of eagerness, half of extreme lassitude, which we find in Botticelli. Only that in Neroni's work it seems not the outcome of a certain dreamy spiritual dissatisfaction—

the dissatisfaction which makes us feel that Botticelli's flower-wreathed nymphs may end in the pool under the willows like Ophelia—but rather of a torturing of line and attitude in search of grace. Grace! Unclutchable phantom, which had appeared tantalisingly in Neroni's recollections of the antique, a something ineffable, which he could not even see clearly when it was there before him, accustomed as he had been to all the hideousness of anatomised reality. In these woodcuts he seems hunting it for ever; and there is one of them which is peculiarly significant, of a nymph in elaborately wound robes and veils, striding, with an odd, mad, uncertain swing, through fields of stiff grass and stunted rushes, a baby faun in her bosom, another tiny goat-legged creature led by the hand, while she carries uncomfortably, in addition to this load, a silly trophy of wild-flowers tied to a stick; the personification almost, this lady with the wide eyes and crazy smile, of the artist's foolishly and charmingly burdened journey in quest of the unattainable. The imaginative quality, never intended or felt by the painter himself, here depends on his embodying longings after the calm and stalwart goddesses on sarcophagus and vase, in the very thing he most seeks to avoid, a creature borrowed from a Botticelli allegory, or one of the sibyls of the unspeakable Perugino himself! The circumstances of this quest, and the accidental meeting in it of the antique and the mediæval, the straining, the Quixote-riding or Three-King pilgrimaging after a phantom, gives to such work of Domenico's that indefinable quality of *charm;* the man does not indeed become a poet, but in a measure a subject for poetry.

III

In order to understand what must have passed in the mind of one of those Florentines of the fifteenth century, we must realise the fact that, unlike ourselves, they had not been brought up under the influence of the antique, and, unlike the ancients, they had not lived in intimacy with Nature. The followers of Giotto had studied little beyond the head and hands, and as much of the body as could be guessed at under drapery or understood from movement; and this achievement, with no artistic traditions save those of the basest Byzantine decay, was far greater than we easily appreciate. It remained for the men of the fifteenth century, Donatello, Ghiberti, Masaccio, and their illustrious followers, to become familiar with the human body. To do so is easy for every one in our day, when we are born, so to speak, with an unconscious habit of antique form, diffused not merely by ancient works of art in marble or plaster, but by more recent schools of art, painting as well as sculpture, themselves the outcome of classical imitation. The early Italian Renaissance had little or none of these facilitations. Fragments of Greek and Roman sculpture were still comparatively uncommon before the great excavations of the sixteenth century; nor was it possible for men so unfamiliar, not merely with the antique, but with Nature itself, to profit very rapidly by the knowledge and taste stored up even in those fragments. It was necessary to learn from reality to appreciate the antique, however much the knowledge of the antique might later supplement, and almost supplant, the study of reality. So these men of the fifteenth century had to teach themselves, in the first instance, the very elements of this knowledge. And here their position, while yet so unlike ours, was even more utterly unlike that of the ancients themselves. The great art of Greece undoubtedly had its days of ignorance; but for those ancient painters and sculptors, who for generations had watched naked lads exercising in the school or racecourse, and draped, half-naked men and women walking in the streets and working in the fields, their ignorance was of the means of representation, not of the object represented. It is the hand, the tool which is at fault in those constrained, simpering warriors of the schools of Ægina, in those slim-waisted dæmonic dancers of the Apulian vases; the eye is as familiar with the human body, the mind as accustomed to select its beauty from its ugliness, as the eye and mind of such of us as cannot paint are familiar nowadays with the shapes and colours, with the charm of the trees and meadows that we love. The contemporaries, on the contrary, of Donatello had received from the sculptors of the very farthest Middle Ages, those who carved the magnificent patterns of

Byzantine coffins and the exquisite leafage of Longobard churches, a remarkable mastery over the technical part of their craft. The hand was cunning, but the eye unfamiliar. Hence it comes that the sculpture of the earlier Renaissance displays perfection of workmanship, which occasionally blinds us to its poverty of form, and even to its deficiency of science. And hence also the rapidity with which every additional item of knowledge is put into practice that seems to argue perfect familiarity. But these men were not really familiar with their work. The dullest modern student, brought up among casts and manuals, would not be guilty of the actual anatomical mistakes committed every now and then by these great anatomists, so passionately curious of internal structure, so exquisitely faithful to minute peculiarity, let alone the bunglings of men so certain of their pencil, so exquisitely keen to form, as Botticelli. As a matter of fact, every statue or drawn figure of this period represents a hard fight with ignorance and with unfamiliarity worse than ignorance. The grosser the failure hard-by, the more splendid the real achievement. For every limb modelled truthfully from the life, every gesture rendered correctly, every bone or muscle making itself felt under the skin, every crease or lump in the surface, is so much conquered from the unknown.

So long as this study, or rather this ignorance, continued, the antique could be appreciated only very partially, and almost exclusively in the points in which it differed least from the works of these modern men. It must have struck them by its unerring science, its great truthfulness to nature, but its superior beauty could not have appealed to artists too unfamiliar with form to think of selecting it.

The study of antique proportion, the reproduction of antique types, so visible in the sculptures of Michelangelo, of Cellini, and of Sansovino, and no less in the painting of Raphael, of Andrea, and even of the later Venetians, was very unimportant in the school of Donatello; and it is probable that he and his pupils did not even perceive the difference between their own works and the old marbles, which they studied merely as so many realistic documents.

During his Florentine days Domenico Neroni, like his masters, was unconscious of the real superiority of the antique, and blind to its difference from what his contemporaries and himself were striving to produce. He did not perceive that the David of Donatello and that of Verrocchio were unlike the marble gods and heroes with whom he would complacently compare them, nor that the bas-reliefs of the divine Ghiberti were far more closely connected with the Gothic work of Orcagna, even of the Pisans, than with those sculptured sarcophagi collected by Cosimo and Piero dei Medici. It was only when his insatiate curiosity had exhausted those problems of anatomy which had still troubled his teachers that he was able to see what the antique really was, or rather to see that the modern was not the same thing. Ghirlandaio, Filippino, Signorelli, and Botticelli undoubtedly were affected by a similar intuition of the Antique; but they were diverted from its thorough investigation by the manifold other problems of painting as distinguished from sculpture, and by the vagueness, the unconsciousness of great creative activity: the antique became one of the influences in their development, helping very quietly to enlarge and refine their work.

It was different with Domenico, in whom the man of science was much more powerful than the artist. His nature required definite decisions and distinct formulas. It took him some time to understand that the school of Donatello differed absolutely from the antique, but the difference once felt, it appeared to him with extraordinary clearness.

He never put his thoughts into words, and probably never admitted even to himself that the works he had most admired were lacking in beauty; he merely asserted that the statues of the old Romans and Greeks were astonishingly beautiful. In reality, however, he was perpetually comparing the two, and always to the disadvantage of the moderns. It is possible in our day to judge justly the comparative merits of antique sculpture and of that of the early Renaissance; or rather to appreciate them as two separate sorts of art, delightful in quite different ways, letting ourselves be charmed not more by the actual beauty of form and nobility of movement of the one than by the simplicity, the very homeliness, the essentially human quality of the other. To us there is something delightful in the very fact that the Davids of Donatello and Verrocchio are mere ordinary striplings from the street and the workshop, that the singers of Luca della Robbia are simple unfledged choir-boys, and the Virgins of Mino Florentine fine ladies; we have enough of antique perfection, we have had too much of pseudo-antique faultlessness, and we feel refreshed by this unconsciousness of beauty and ugliness. A contemporary could not enter into such feelings, he could not enjoy his own and his fellows' *naïveté;* besides, the antique was only just becoming manifest, and therefore triumphant. To Domenico, Donatello's David became more and more unsatisfactory, faulty above the waist, positively ungainly below, weak and lubberly; how could so divine an artist have been satisfied with that flat back, those narrow shoulders and thick thighs? He felt freer to dislike the work of Verrocchio, his own teacher, and a man without Donatello's overwhelming genius; that David of his, with his immense head and wizen face, his pitiful child's arms and projecting clavicles, straddling with hand on hip; was it possible that a great hero, the slayer of a giant (Domenico's notions of giants were taken rather from the romances of chivalry recited in the market than from study of Scripture) should have been made like that? And so, like his great contemporary Mantegna in far-off Lombardy,

Domenico turned that eager curiosity with which he had previously sought for the secret of flayed limbs and fleshless skeletons, to studying the mystery of proportion and beauty which was hidden, more subtly and hopelessly, in the broken marbles of the Pagans.

It happened one day, somewhere about the year 1485, that he was called to examine a group of Bacchus and a Faun, recently brought from Naples by the banker Neri Altoviti, of the family which once owned a charming house, recently destroyed, whose triple row of pillared balconies used to put an odd Florentine note into the Papal Rome, turning the swirl of the Tiber opposite Saint Angelo's into a reach of the Arno. The houses of the Altovitis in Florence were in that portion of the town most favoured by the fifteenth century, already a little way from the market: the lion on the tower of the Podestà, and the Badia steeple printing the sky close by; while not far off was the shop where the good bookseller Vespasiano received orders for manuscripts, and conversed with the humanists whose lives he was to write. The Albizis and Pandolfinis, illustrious and numerous families, struck in so many of their members by the vindictiveness of the Medicis, had their houses in the same quarter, and at the corner of the narrow street hung the carved escutcheon—two fishes rampant—of the Pazzis: their house shut up and avoided by the citizens, who had so recently seen the conspirators dangling in hood and cape from the windows of the public palace. The house of the Altovitis was occupied on the ground floor by great warehouses, whose narrow, grated windows were attainable only by a steep flight of steps. The court was surrounded on three sides by a cloister or portico, which repeated itself on the first and second floors, with the difference that the lowest arches were supported by rude square pillars, ornamented with only a carved marigold, while the uppermost weighed on stout oaken shafts, between which ropes were stretched for the drying of linen ; and the middle colonnade consisted of charming Tuscan columns, where Sirens and Cupids and heraldic devices replaced the acanthus or rams' horns of the capitals. It was to this middle portion of the house that Domenico ascended up a noble steep-stepped staircase, protected from the rain by a vaulted and rosetted roof, for it was external and occupied the side of the yard left free from cloisters. The great banker had bidden Domenico to his midday meal, which was served with a frugality now fast disappearing, but once habitual even among the richest Florentines. But though the food was simple and almost scanty, nearly forty persons sat down to meat together, for Neri Altoviti held to the old plan, commended by Alberti in his dialogue on the governing of a household, that the clerks and principal servants of a merchant were best chosen among his own kinsfolk, living under his roof, and learning obedience from the example of his children. Despite this frugality, the dining-room was, though bare, magnificent. There were none of those carpets and Eastern stuffs which surprised strangers from the North in the voluptuous little palaces of contemporary Venetians, and the benches were hard and narrow. But the ceiling overhead was magnificently arranged in carved compartments, great gold sunflowers and cherubs projecting from a dark blue ground among the brown raftering; in the middle of the stencilled wall was one of those high sideboards so frequently shown in old paintings, covered with gold and silver dishes and platters embossed by the most skilful craftsmen; and at one end a great washing trough and fountain, such as still exist in sacristies, ornamented with groups of dancing children by Benedetto da Maiano; while behind the high seat of the father of the family a great group of saints, emerging from blooming lilies and surrounded by a glory of angels, was hanging in a frame divided into carved compartments: the work, panel and frame, of the late Brother Filippo Lippi. At one end of the board sat all the men, arranged hierarchically, from the father in his black loose robe to lads in short plaited tunic and striped hose; the womankind were seated together, and the daughters, even the mother of the house, modest and almost nunlike in apparel and head-dress, would rise and help to wait on the men, with that silent and grave courtesy which, according to Vespasiano, had disappeared from Florence with Alessandra dei Bardi. There was little speech, and only in undertones; a Franciscan said a long grace, and afterwards, and in the middle of the meal, a young student, educated by the frequent munificence of the Altovitis, read out loud a chapter of Cicero's " De Senectute;" for Neri, although a busy banker, with but little time for study, was not behind his generation in the love of letters and philosophy.

After meat Messer Neri dismissed the rest of the company to their various avocations; the ladies silently retired to superintend the ironing and mending of the house linen, and Domenico was escorted by his host to see the newly arrived piece of statuary. It had been placed already in the banker's closet, where he could feast his eyes on its perfection while attending to his business or improving his mind by study. This closet, compared to the rest of the house, was small and low-roofed. At its end, as we see in the pictures of Van Eyck and Memling, opened out the conjugal chamber, reflecting its vast, red-covered bed, raised several steps, its crucifix and praying-stool, and its latticed window in a circular mirror framed in cut facets, which hung opposite on the wall of the closet. The latter was dark, a single trefoiled window admitting on either side of its column and through its greenish bottle-glass but little light from the narrow street. The chief furniture consisted of shelves carrying books, small antique bronzes, some globes, a sand-glass, and panel cupboards, ornamented with pictures of similar objects, and with ingenious perspectives of inlaid wood. An elaborate iron safe, painted blue and studded with beautiful metal roses, stood in a corner. There were two or three arm-chairs of carved oak for visitors. The master sat upon a bench behind an oaken counter or desk, very much like St. Jerome in his study. On the wall behind, and above his head, hung a precious Flemish painting (Flemish paintings were esteemed for their superior devoutness) representing the Virgin at the foot of the Cross, with a Nativity and a Circumcision on either of the opened shutters. It made a glowing patch of vivid geranium and wine colour, of warm yellow glazing on the oak of the wall. On the counter or writing-table stood a majolica pot with three lilies in it, a pile of manuscript and ledgers, and a human skull alongside of a crucifix, beautifully wrought of bronze by Desiderio da Settignano. A Latin translation of Plato's "Phædo" was spread open on the desk, together with one of the earliest printed copies of the "Divine Comedy."

Messer Neri did not take his seat at the counter, but, after a pause, and with some solemnity, drew a curtain of dark brocade which had been spread across one end of the closet, and displayed his new purchase.

"I have it from the king, for the settling of a debt of a thousand crowns contracted with my father, when he was Duke of Calabria," said the banker, with due appreciation of the sum. "'Tis said they found it among the ruins of that famous palace of the Emperor Tiberius of which Tacitus has told us."

The two marble figures, to which time and a long sojourn underground had given a brownish yellow colour, reddish in places with rust stains, stood out against a background of Flemish tapestry, whose emaciated heads of kings and thin bodies of warrior saints made a confused pattern on the general dusky blue and green. The group was in wonderful preservation: the figure of Bacchus intact, that of the young faun lacking only the arm, which had evidently been freely extended.

It exists in many repetitions and variations in most of our museums; a work originally of the school of Praxiteles, but in none of the copies handed to us of excellence sufficient to display the hand of the original sculptor. Besides, we have been spoilt by familiarity with an older and more powerful school, by knowledge of a few great masterpieces, for complete appreciation of such a work. But it was different four hundred years ago; and Domenico Neroni stood long and entranced before the group. The principal figure embodied all those beauties which he had been striving so hard to understand: it was, in the most triumphant manner, the absolute reverse of the figures of Donatello.

The young god was represented walking with leisurely but vigorous step, supporting himself upon the shoulder of the little satyr as the vine supports itself, with tendrils trailed about branches and trunk, on the propping tree from which the child Ampelos took his name. Like the head with its elaborately dressed curls, the beautiful body had an ampleness and tenderness that gave an impression almost womanly till you noticed the cuirass-like sit of the chest on the loins, and the compressed strength of the long light thighs. The creature, as you looked at him, seemed to reveal more and more, beneath the roundness and fairness of surface, the elasticity and strength of an athlete in training. But when the eye was not exploring the delicate, hard, and yet supple depressions and swellings of the muscles, the slender shapeliness of the long legs and springy feet, the back bulging with strong muscles above, and going in, tight, with a magnificent dip at the waist; all impressions were merged in a sense of ease, of suavity, of full-blown harmony. Here was no pomp of anatomical lore, of cunning handicraft, but the life seemed to circulate strong and gentle in this exquisite effortless body. And the creature was not merely alive with a life more harmonious than that of living men or carved marbles, but beautiful, equally in simple outline if you chose that, and in subtle detail when that came under your notice, with a beauty that seemed to multiply itself, existing in all manners, as it can only in things that have life, in perfect flowers and fruits, or high-bred Oriental horses. Of such things did the under-strata of consciousness consist in Neroni—vague impressions of certain bunches of grapes with their great rounded leaves hanging against the blue sky, of the flame-like tapered petals of wild tulips in the fields, of the golden brown flanks of certain horses, and the broad white foreheads of the Umbrian bullocks; forming as it were a background for the perception of this god, for no man or woman had ever been like unto him.

Domenico remained silent, his arms folded on his breast; it was not a case for talking.

But the young man who had read Cicero aloud at table had come up behind him, and thought it more seemly to praise his patron's new toy, while at the same time displaying his learning; so he cleared his throat, and said in a pompous manner:—

"It is stated in the fifth chapter of the Geography of Strabo that the painter Parrhasius, having been summoned by the inhabitants of Lindos to make them an image of their tutelary hero Hercules, obtained from the son of Jupiter that he should appear to him in a dream, and thus enable him worthily to portray the perfections of a demigod. Might we not be tempted to believe that the divine son of Semele had vouchsafed a similar boon to the happy sculptor of this marble?"

But Domenico only bit his thumb and sighed very heavily.

IV

To the men of those days, which have taken their name from the revival of classical studies, Antiquity, although studied and aped till its phrases, feelings, and thoughts had entered familiarly into all life, remained, nevertheless, a period of permanent miracle. It was natural, therefore, to the contemporaries of Poggius and Æneas

Sylvius, of Ficinus and Politian, that the art of the Romans and Greeks should, like their poetry, philosophy, and even their virtues, be of transcendent and unqualified splendour. Why it should be thus they asked as little as why the sun shines, mediæval men as they really were, and accepting quite simply certain phenomena as the result of inscrutable virtues. Even later, when Machiavelli began to examine why the ancients had been more valorous and patriotic than his contemporaries, nay, when Montaigne expounded with sceptical cynicism the superior sanity and wisdom of Pagan days, people were satisfied to think—when they thought at all—that antique art was excellent because it belonged to antiquity. And it was not till the middle of the eighteenth century that the genius of Winkelmann brought into fruitful contact the study of ancient works of art, and that of the manners and notions of antiquity, showing the influence of a civilisation which cultivated bodily beauty as an almost divine quality, and making us see behind that beautiful nation of marble the generations of living athletes, among whom the sculptor had found his critics and his models.

To a man like Domenico Neroni, devoid of classical learning and accustomed to struggling with anatomy and perspective, the problem of ancient art was not settled by the fact of its antiquity. He had gone once more to Rome on purpose to see as many old marbles as possible, and he brought to their study the feverish curiosity with which in former years he had flayed and cut up corpses and spent his nights in calculations of perspective. To such a mind, where modern scientific methods were arising among mediæval habits of allegory and mysticism, the statues and reliefs which he was perpetually analysing became a sort of subsidiary nature, whose riddles might be read by other means than mere investigation; for do not the forces of Nature, its elemental spirits, give obedience to wonderful words and potent combinations of numbers?

Certain significant facts had flashed across his mind in his studies of that almost abstract, nay, almost cabalistic thing, the science of bodily proportions. It was plain that the mystery of antique beauty—the ancient symmetry, *symmetria prisca* as a humanist designs it in his epitaph for Leonardo da Vinci—was but a matter of numbers. For a man's length, if he stand with outstretched arms, is the same from finger tip to finger tip as his length when erect from head to feet, namely, eight times the length of his head. Now eight heads, if divided into halves, give four as the measure of throat and thorax; and four heads to the length of the leg from the acetabulum to the heel, divided themselves into two heads going to the thigh and two heads to the shank; while in the cross measurement two heads equal the breadth of the chest, and three measure the length from the shoulder to the middle finger. These measures—a mere rough rule of thumb in our eyes—contained to this mediæval mind the promise of some great mystery. To him, accustomed to hear all the occurrences of Nature, and all human concerns referred to astrological calculations, and conceiving the universe as governed by spirits—in shape, perhaps, like the Primum Mobile, the Mercurius and Jupiter of Mantegna's playing cards, crowned with stars and poised upon globes— it was as if the divining rod were turning pertinaciously to one spot in the earth, where, had he but the necessary tools, he must strike upon veins of the purest gold, or cause water to spirt high in the air. This number *eight*, and the pertinacity of its recurrence, puzzled him intensely. It seemed to point so clearly, much as in music the sensitive seventh points to the tonic, to a sort of resolution on the number nine. And if only nine could be established, it would seem to explain so much. . . . For five being man's numeral in creation (and is not the measurement of his face also *five eyes?*), it makes, when added to four, the number of the material elements over which he dominates, *nine*, which would thus represent the supremacy or perfection of man. Man's power of reproduction being represented by three, its multiple nine would be still more obviously important. How to turn this eight into nine became Domenico's study, and he took measurement after measurement for this purpose. At length he remembered that man's body is a unity, therefore represented by the number one, and that will, judgment, and supremacy are also comprised in the unit. Now one and eight make nine beyond all possibility of doubt, and the formula—" man's body is a unity—or one "—composed of harmonies of eight, would give the formula *nine* meaning *man's supremacy is expressed in his body*. The importance of working round to this famous nine will be clear when we reflect that, according to the Kabbala and the lost sacred book of Hermes Trismegistus—the Pimandra, doubtless, which he is represented, on the floor of Siena Cathedral, as offering to a Jew and a Gentile—nine represents the sun and all beautiful bright things that draw their influence from it, as the gleam of beaten gold, the rustle of silken stuffs, the smell of the flower heliotrope, and all such men as delineate human beings with colours, or make their effigy in stone or metal; moreover, Phœbus Apollo, whom the poets describe as the most beautiful of the gods, as indeed he is represented in all statues and reliefs.

Domenico would often discuss these matters with a learned man who greatly frequented his company. This was the humanist Niccolò Feo, known as Filarete. Filarete was a native of Southern Apulia, a bastard of the house of the Counts of Sulmona, who, in order to prevent any plots against the legitimate branch, had handsomely provided for him in an abbey of which they enjoyed the patronage. But his restless spirit drove him from the cloister, and impelled him to long and adventurous journeys. He had travelled in India and the East, and in Greece, returning to Italy only when Constantinople fell before the Turks. During these years he had acquired immense learning, considerable wealth, and a vaguely sinister reputation. He had been persecuted by Paul II. for taking part in the famous banquets, savouring oddly of Paganism, of Pomponius Lætus; but the late Pontiff Sixtus IV. had taken him into his favour together with Platina, one of his fellow-sufferers in the castle of Saint Angelo. He was now old, and, after a life of study, adventure, and possibly of sin, was living in affluence in a house given him by the illustrious Cardinal at St. Peter ad Vinculas, who had also obtained him a canonry of St. John Lateran. He was busying his last year in a great work of fancy and erudition, for which he required the assistance of a skilful draughtsman and connoisseur of antiquities, than whom none could suit him so well as Domenico Neroni.

The book of Filarete, of which the rare copies are among the most precious relics of the Renaissance, was a strange mixture of romance, allegory, and encyclopædic knowledge, such as had been common in the Middle Ages, and was still fashionable during the revival of letters, which merely added the element of classical learning. Like the *Hypnerotomachia Poliphili* of Francesco Colonna, of which it was doubtless the prototype, the *Alcandros* of Filarete, though never carried beyond the first volume, is an amazing and wearisome display of the author's archæological learning. It contains exact descriptions of all the rarities of ancient art, and of things Oriental which he had seen, and pages of transcripts from obscure Latin and Greek authors, descriptive of religious ceremonies; varied with Platonic philosophy, Decameronian obscenities, in laboured pseudo-Florentine style, and Dantesque visions, all held together by the confused narrative of an allegorical journey performed by the author. It is profusely ornamented with woodcuts, representing architectural designs of a fantastic, rather Oriental description, restorations of ancient buildings, reproductions of antique inscriptions and designs, and last, but far from least, a certain number of small compositions, of Mantegnesque quality, but Botticellian charm, showing the various adventures of the hero in terrible woods, delicious gardens, and in the company of nymphs, demigods, and allegorical personages. These latter are undoubtedly from the hand of Domenico Neroni; and it was while discussing these delightful damsels seated with lutes and psalteries under vine-trellises, these scholars in cap and gown, weeping in quaint chambers with canopied beds and carnations growing on the window, these processions—suggesting Mantegna's Triumph of Julius Cæsar—of priests and priestesses with victories and trophies, that the painter from Volterra and the Apulian humanist would discuss the secret of antique beauty—discuss it for hours, surrounded by the precious manuscripts and inscriptions, the fragments of sculpture, the Eastern rarities, of Filarete's little house on the Quirinal hill, or among the box-hedges, clipped cypresses, and fountains of his garden; while the riots and massacres, the fanatical processions and feudal wars, of mediæval Rome raged unnoticed below. For Pope Sixtus and his Riarios, and Pope Innocent and his Cybos, thirsting for power and gold, drunken with lust and bloodshed, were benign and courteous patrons of all art and all learning.

V

But that number nine, attained with so much difficulty, although it put the human proportion into visible connection with the sun, with beaten gold, the smell of the heliotrope, and the god Apollo, and opened a vista of complicated astral influences, did not in reality bring Domenico one step nearer the object of his desires. It had enabled those ancient men to make statues that were perfectly beautiful, that was obvious; but it did not make his own figures one tittle less hideous, for he felt them now to be absolutely hideous. One wintry day, as he was roaming amongst the fallen pillars and arches, thickly covered with myrtle and ilex, of the desolate region beyond what had once been the Forum and was now the cattle-market, there came across Domenico's mind, while he watched a snake twisting in the grass, the remembrance of a certain anecdote about a Greek painter, to whom Hercules had shown himself in a vision. He had heard it, without taking any notice, two years before, from the young scholar who read Cicero at table for Messer Neri Altoviti; and although he had thought of it several times, it had never struck him except as one of the usual impudent displays of learning of the parasitic tribe of humanists.

But at this moment the remembrance of this fact came as a great light into Domenico's soul. For what were these statues save the idols of the heathens; and what wonder they should be divinely beautiful, when those who made them might see the gods in visions?

This explanation, which to us must sound far-fetched and fantastic, knowing, as we do, the real reason that made a people of athletes into a people of sculptors, savoured of no strangeness to a man of the Middle Ages. Visions of superhuman creatures were among the most undisputed articles of his belief, and among the commonest subjects of his art. Had not the Blessed Virgin appeared to St. Bernard, the Saviour among His cherubim to St. Francis—the very stones shown at La Vernia where it had happened—the Divine Bridegroom to Catherine of Siena? Had not St. Anthony of Padua held the Divine Child in his arms? And all not so long ago? Besides, every year there was some nun or monk claiming to have conversed with Christ and His court; and the heavens were opening quite frequently in the walls of cells and the clefts of hermitages. And did not Dante relate a journey into Hell, Purgatory, and Paradise? It was perfectly natural that what was constantly happening to holy men and women nowadays should have happened in Pagan times also; and what men could so well have deserved a visit from gods as those who spent their lives faithfully portraying them? The story of Parrhasius and his vision was familiar ground to a man accustomed to see, in all corners of Italy, portraits of the Saviour painted by St. Luke, or finished, like the famous Holy Face of Lucca, by angels. For an absolute contempt for the artistic value of such miraculous images did not, in the mind of Neroni, throw any doubt on their authenticity; in the same way that the passion for antiquity, the hankering after Pagan beliefs, did not probably interfere with the orthodoxy of so many of the humanists. Domenico, besides, remembered that Virgil and Ovid, whom he had not read, but whose fables he had sometimes been asked to illustrate, were constantly talking of visions of gods and goddesses, nay, of their descending upon earth to unite themselves with mortals in love or friendship, for he had had to furnish designs for woodcuts representing Diana and Endymion, Jupiter and Ganymede, the gods coming to Philemon and Baucis, and Apollo tending the herds of Admetus. Neither did it occur to Domenico's mind that the existence of the old gods might be a mere invention, or a mere delusion of the heathen. For all their classic culture, the men of the fifteenth century, as the men of the thirteenth for all their scholasticism, were in an intellectual condition such as we rarely meet with nowadays among educated persons; and Domenico, a mere handicraftsman, had not learned from the study of Cicero and Plato to examine and understand the difference between reality and fiction. To him a scene which was frequently painted, an adventure which was written down and could be read, was necessarily a reality. Dante had spoken of the gods, and what Dante said was evidently true, the allegorical meaning, the metaphor, entirely escaping this simple mind; and Virgil, Homer, Ovid told the most minute details about gods and goddesses, and they themselves were grave and learned men. Domenico did not even think that the ancient gods were dead. Of course heaven was now occupied by Christ and His saints, those heavenly hosts of whom he would think, when he thought of them at all, as seated stepwise on a great stand, blue and pink and green in dress, golden discs about their heads, and an atmosphere of fretted gold, of swirling stencilled golden angels' wings all round them, and God the Father, a great triangle blazing with Alpha and Omega, above Jesus enthroned, and His mother; and it was they who ruled things here, and to them he said his prayers night and morning, and knelt in church. But *here*, somehow did not cover the whole universe, nor did that pink and blue and gold miniature painter's heaven extend everywhere, although, of course, somehow or other it did. Anyhow, it was certain that not so very far off there were Saracens and Turks—why he had seen some of the Duke of Calabria's Turkish garrison—who believed in Macomet, Trevigant, and Apollinis; these to be sure were false gods (the word *false* carried no clear meaning to his mind, or if any, one rather equivalent to *wrong, objectionable* rather than to non-existent), but they certainly worked wonderful miracles for their people. And indeed—here Domenico's placid contemplation of the kingdom of Macomet, Trevigant, and Apollinis was exchanged for a vague horror, shot with gleams of curiosity—the devil also had his place in the world, a place much nearer and universal, and did marvellous things, pointing out treasures, teaching the future, lending invulnerable strength to the men and women who worshipped him, of whom some might be pointed out to you in every town—yes, grave and respectable men, priests and monks among them, and even Cardinals of Holy Church, as every one knew quite well. . . . So that, in a confused manner, rather negative than positive, Domenico considered that the Pagan gods must be somewhere or other, the past and present not very clearly separated in his mind, or rather the past existing in a peculiar simultaneous manner with the present, as a sort of St. Brandan's isle, in distant, unattainable seas; or as Dante's mountain of Purgatory, a very solid mountain indeed, yet which, for some mysterious and unquestioned reason, people never stumbled upon except after death. All this was scarcely an actual series of arguments; it was rather the arguments which, with much effort, Domenico might have fished out of his obscure consciousness had you summoned him to explain how the ancient gods could possibly be immortal. As to him, he had always heard of them as immortal, and although he had not been taught any respect or love for them as for Christ, the Madonna, and the saints, they must be existing somewhere since *immortal* means that which cannot die.

But now he began to feel a certain shyness about immortal gods, for they had begun to occupy his thoughts, and it was with much cunning that he put questions to his friend Filarete, desirous to gain information on certain points without actually seeming to ask it. The humanist, summoned to explain what the Fathers of the Church—those worthies crowned with mitres and offering rolls of manuscript, whom Domenico had occasionally to portray for his customers—said about the ancient gods, answered with much glibness but considerable contempt, for the Greek and Latin of these saintly philosophers inspired the learned man with a feeling of nausea. He got out of a chest several volumes covered with dust, and began to quote the "Apology" of Justin Martyr, the "Legation" of Athenagoras, the "Apology" of Tertullian and Lactantius, whose very name caused him to writhe with philological loathing. And he told Domenico that it was the opinion of these holy but ill-educated persons that dæmons assumed the name and attributes of Jupiter, of Venus, of Apollo and Bacchus, lurking in temples, instituting festivals and sacrifices, and were often allowed by Heaven to distract the faithful by a display of miracles.

"Then they are devils?" asked Domenico, trying to follow.

A smile passed over the beautifully cut mouth, the noble, wrinkled face—like that of the marble Seneca —of the old humanist.

"Talk of devils to the barefoot friar who preaches in the midst of the market-place," he said, "not to Filarete. The whole world, air, fire, earth, water, the entire universe is governed by dæmons, and they inspire our noblest thoughts. Hast never heard of the familiar dæmon of Socrates, whispering to him superhuman wisdom? Yes, indeed, Venus, Apollo, Æsculapius, Jove, the stars and planets, the winds and tides are dæmons. But thou canst not understand such matters, my poor Domenico. So get thee to Brother Baldassare of Palermo, and ask him questions."

But Filarete's expression was very different when, one day, Domenico shyly inquired concerning the truth of that story of Parrhasius and the Hercules of Lindos. Strange rumours were current in Rome of unholy festivities in which Filarete and other learned men—some of those whom Paul II. had thrown into prison—had once taken part. They had not merely laid their tables and spread their couches according to descriptions contained in ancient authors; but, crowned with roses, laurel, myrtle, or parsley, had sung hymns to the heathen gods, and, it was whispered, poured out libations and burned incense in their honour. Their friends, indeed, had answered scornfully that these were but amusements of learned men; not to be taken more seriously than the invocations to the gods and muses in their poems, than the mythological subjects which the Popes themselves selected to adorn their dwellings. And doubtless this explanation was correct. Yet the pleasure of these little pedantic and artistic mummeries, which took place in suburban gardens, while the townsfolk streamed in the hot June nights, decked with bunches of cloves and of lavender, to make bonfires in the empty places near the Lateran, little guessing that their ancestors had once done the same in honour of the neighbouring Venus—the innocent childishness of these learned men was perhaps spiced, for some individuals at least, by a momentary belief in the gods of the old poets, by a sudden forbidden fervour for the exiled divinities of Virgil and Ovid, under whose reign the world had been young, men had been free to love and think, and Rome, now the object of the world's horror and contempt, had been the world's triumphant mistress. But these had been mere mummeries, mere child's play, and the soul of Filarete had thirsted for a reality. He could not have answered had you asked whether he believed in the absolute existence and power of the old gods, any more than whether he disbelieved in the power of Christ and His avenging angels; his cultivated and sceptical mind was, after all, in a state of disorder similar to that of Domenico's ignorance. All that he knew with certainty was that Christ and His worship represented to him all that was unnatural, cruel, foolish, and hypocritical; while the gods were associated with every thought of liberty, of beauty, and of glory. And so, one evening, after working up still further the enthusiasm, the passionate desire of his friend, he told Domenico that, if he chose, he too perhaps might see a god.

In his antiquarian rambles Filarete had discovered, a mile or two outside the southern gates of Rome, a subterranean chamber, richly adorned with stuccoes—known nowadays as the tomb of certain members of the Flavian family, but which, thanks to the defective knowledge of his day and the habit of seeing people buried in churches, the humanist had mistaken for a temple—intact, and scarcely desecrated, of the Eleusinian Bacchus. Above its vaults, barely indicated by a higher mound in the waving ground of the pasture land, had once stood a Christian church, as ancient almost as the supposed temple below, whose Byzantine columns lay half hidden by the high grass, and the walls of whose apse had become overgrown by ivy and weeds, the nest of lazy snakes. The Gothic soldiers, Arians or heathens, who had burned down, in some drunken bout, the little church above-ground, had penetrated at the same time into the tomb beneath in search of treasure, and finding none, dispersed the bones in the sarcophagi they had opened. They had left open the aperture leading downward, which had been matted over by a thick growth of ivy and wild clematis. One day, while surveying the remains of the Christian church, always in hopes of discovering in it a former temple of the Pagans, Filarete had walked into that tuft of solid green, and found himself, buried and half stunned, in the mouth of the tomb below. It was through this that he bade Domenico follow him, bearing a certain mysterious package in his cloak, one January day of the year fourteen hundred and eighty-eight.

Above-ground it had frozen in the night; here below, when they had descended the rugged sepulchral stairs, the air had a damp warmth, an odd feel of inhabitation. Above-ground, also, everything lay in ruins, while here all was intact. As the light of the torches moved slowly along the vaulted and stuccoed ceilings, it showed the delicate lines of a profusion of little reliefs and ornaments, fresh as if cast and coloured yesterday. Slender garlands of leaves, and long knotted ribbons and veils in lowest relief partitioned the space; and framed by them, now round, now oval, now oblong, were medallions of naked gods banqueting and playing games, of satyrs and nymphs dancing, nereids swinging on the backs of hippocamps, tritons curling their tails and blowing their horns, Cupids fluttering among griffins and chimæras; a life of laughter and love, which mocked the eye, starting into vividness in one place, dying away in a mere film where the torchlight pressed on too closely in others. All along the walls, below the line of the stuccoes, were excavated shelves, on which stood numbers of small cinerary boxes, each bearing a name. In the middle of the vaulted chamber was a huge stone coffin, carved with revelling Bacchantes, and grim tragic masks at its corners; and all round the coffin, broken in one of its flanks by the tools of the treasure-seeker, lay bones and skulls, dispersed on the damp ground even as the Goths had left them.

It was this sarcophagus which, with its Dionysiac revels, and the name of one Dionysius carved on it, a freedman of the Flavians, had led Filarete to consider the tomb as a kind of temple consecrated to Bacchus.

Filarete bade Domenico stick the pointed end of his torch into the mouth of an amphora standing erect in a corner, and began to unpack the load they had brought on a mule. It looked like the preparation for a feast: there were loaves of bread, fruit, a flask of choice wine; and Domenico, for a moment, thought the old man mad. But his feelings changed when Filarete produced a set of silver lamps, and bade him trim and light them, placing them on the ledges alongside of the cinerary urns; and when he lit some strange incense and filled the place with its smoke. Despite the many descriptions of ancient sacrifices with which the humanist had entertained him, Domenico had brought a vague notion of a raising of devils, and felt relieved at the absence of brimstone fumes, and of the magic books that accompanied them.

Although more passionately longing—he knew not, he dared not tell himself for what—Domenico did not come with the curious exaltation of spirits of his companion, all whose antiquarian lore had gone to his head, and who really imagined himself to be a genuine

Pagan engaged in Pagan rites. For Filarete the ceremony was everything; for Domenico it was merely a means, a sort of sacrilegious juggling, into which he had not inquired more particularly, which was to give him the object of his wishes at the price of great peril to his soul. But when the subterranean chamber was filled with a cloud of incense, through which, in the dim yellow light of the lamp, the naked gods and goddesses on the vault, the satyrs and nymphs, the Tritons and Bacchantes seemed to float in and out of sight, a feeling of awe, of an unknown kind of reverence and rapture, began to fill his soul, and his eyes became fixed on the lid of the carved sarcophagus—vague images of Christian resurrections mingling with his hopes—Would the god appear?

Filarete, meanwhile, had enveloped his head in a long linen veil, and, after washing his hands thrice in a golden basin brought for the purpose, he placed some faggots on the sarcophagus, lit them, and throwing grains of incense and of salt alternately into the flames, began to chant in an unknown tongue, which Domenico guessed to be Greek. Then beckoning to the painter, who was kneeling, as at church, in a corner, he bade him unpack a basket matted over with leaves, whose movements and sounds had puzzled Domenico as he carried it down. In great surprise, and with a vague sense of he knew not what, he handed its contents to Filarete. It was a miserable little lamb, newly born, its long, soft legs tied together, its almost sightless, pale eyes half-started from its sockets. As the humanist took it, it bleated with sudden shrill strength, and Domenico could not help thinking of certain images he had seen on monastery walls of the Good Shepherd carrying the lame lamb on his shoulders. This was very different. For, with an odd ferocity, Filarete placed the miserable young creature on the stone before the fire, and slit its throat and chest with a long knife.

The god did not appear. They extinguished the lamps, left the carcase of the lamb half charred in a pool of blood on the stone, and slowly reascended into the daylight, leaving behind them, in the vaulted chamber, a stifling fume of incense, of burnt flesh, and mingled damp.

Up above, among the ruins of the Christian church, where they had left their mules, it was cold and sunny, and the light seemed curiously blue, almost grey and dusty, after the yellow illumination below. Before them, interrupted here and there by a mass of ruined masonry, or a few arches of aqueduct, waved the grey-green, billowy plain, where the wind, which rolled the great winter cloud-balls overhead, danced and sang with the tall, dry hemlocks and sere white thistles, shining and rattling like skeletons. And on to it seemed to descend cloud-mountains, vague blueness and darkness—cloud or hill, you could not tell which—out of whose flank, ever and anon, a sunbeam conjured up a visionary white resplendent city.

The short winter day was beginning to draw in when they approached silently the city walls, solemn with their towers and gates, endless as it seemed, and enclosing, one felt vaguely, an endless, distant, invisible city.

The sound of its bells came as from afar to meet the sacrilegious men.

VI

The culminating sacrilege was yet to come. The place that witnessed it remains unchanged—a half-deserted church among the silent grass-grown lanes, the crumbling convent walls, and ill-tended vineyards of the Aventine; a hill that has retained in Christian times a look of its sinister fame in Pagan ones. Among the cypresses, which seem to wander up the hillside, rises the square belfry, among whose brickwork, flushed in the sunset, are inlaid discs of porphyry torn from some temple pavement, and plates of green majolica brought from the East, it is said, by pilgrims or Crusaders. The arum-fringed lane widens before the outer wall of the church, overtopped by its triangular gable. Behind this wall is a yard or atrium, the pavement grass-grown, the walls stained with great patches of mildew, and showing here and there in their dilapidation the shaft and capital of a bricked-up Ionic pillar. The place tells of centuries of neglect, of the gradual invasion of resistless fever; and it was fitly chosen, some fifty years ago, for the abode of a community of Trappists. In the reign of Innocent VIII. it was still nominally in the hands of certain Cistercians; but the fever had long driven these monks to the more wholesome end of the hill, where they had erected a smaller church; and the convent had served for years as a fortress of the turbulent family of the Capranicas, one of whose members was always the nominal abbot, with the Cardinal's hat, and title Jervase and Protasius. And now, at the end of the fifteenth century, a Cardinal Ascanio Capranica, famous for his struggle in magnificence and sinfulness with the magnificent and sinful young nephews of Pope Sixtus, had determined to restore the fortified monastery, to combat the fever by abundant plantations, and to make the church a monument of his splendour. And, in order to secure some benefit by his own munificence, he had begun by commissioning Domenico Neroni to design and execute a sepulchre three storeys high, full of carvings, and covered with statues, so that his soul, if sent untimely to heaven, might not be dishonoured by the unworthy resting-place of its trusty companion, the Cardinal's handsome and well-tended body.

This church of SS. Jervase and Protasius, which imitated, like most churches of the early Christian period, the form of a basilica or court of law, was constructed out of fragments of Pagan edifices, and occupied the site of a Pagan edifice, whose columns had been employed to carry the roof of the church, or, when of porphyry or serpentine, had been sawed into discs for the pavement. On the slant of the hill, supporting the apse, encircled by pillarets, is a round mass of masonry, overgrown with ivy and ilex scrub, the remains of some antique bath or grotto; and under the battlemented walls, the cloistered courts of the convent, there stretches, it is said, a network of subterranean passages running down to the Tiber. Four hundred years ago they were not to be discovered if looked for, being completely hidden by the fallen masonry and the cypress roots and growths of poisonous plants—nightshade, and hemlock, and green-flowered hellebore; but wicked monks had sometimes been sucked into them while digging the ground, or decoyed into their labyrinths by devils. Was it possible that there had lingered on through the ages a vague and horrified remembrance of those rites, the discovery of whose mysterious and wide-spread abominations had frozen Rome with horror in her most high and palmy days; and was there a connection between those neophytes, wandering with blood-stained limbs and dishevelled locks among the groves of the Aventine, then rushing to quench their burning torches in the Tiber, two centuries before Christ, and the devils who troubled the Benedictines of SS. Jervase and Protasius? These evil spirits would appear, it had been said, in the cloisters of the convent, processions carrying lights and garlands; and on certain nights, when the monks were in prayer in their cells, strange sounds would issue from the church itself, of flutes and timbrels, and demon laughter, and demon voices chanting some unknown litany, and clearly aping the mass; and Cardinal Capranica was blamed by many pious persons for his rash intention of filling once more the deserted convent, and exposing holy men to the wrath of such very pertinacious devils. Meanwhile mass upon mass was said to clear the place of this demoniac infection. In was in this church that the sacrilege of Domenico and Filarete rose to its highest, and that an event took place which the men of the fifteenth century could scarce find words to designate.

Domenico had grown tired of his friend's archæological impieties. It gave him no satisfaction to pour out wine, burn incense, arrange garlands, and even cut the throats of animals according to a correct Pagan ritual. It was nothing to him that Horace and Ovid and Tibullus should have done alike. He was a good Christian, never doubting for a moment the power of the Blessed Virgin, the saints, and even the smallest and meanest priest, nor the heat of hell-fire. But he wanted to have the secret of antique proportions, and he was convinced that this secret could be communicated only by a Pagan divinity, just as certain theological mysteries, such as the use of the rosary, had been revealed to the saints by Christ or the Virgin. The Pagan gods were devils, and to hold communication with devils was mortal sin and sure damnation. But lots of people communicated with devils for much more paltry motives, for greed of gold or love of woman;

and were yet saved by the intercession of some heavenly patron, or found it worth while not to be saved at all. Domenico, like them, put the question of salvation behind him. He might think of that afterwards, when he had possessed himself of the proportion of the ancients. At all events, at present he was willing to risk everything in order to attain that. He was determined to see that god of the heathens, not as he had seen him once in the house of Messer Neri Altoviti, cut out of marble, but alive, moving, speaking; for *that* was the god.

The god was a devil. Now it is well known that there is a way of compelling every devil to show himself, providing you use sufficiently strong spells. They had sacrificed goats and lambs enough, also doves, and had burned perfumes, and spilt wine sufficient for one of Cardinal Riario's suppers. It was evidently not that sort of sacrifice which would rejoice the god or compel him to show himself. For weeks and weeks Domenico ruminated over the subject. And little by little the logical, inevitable answer dawned upon his horrified but determined mind. For what was the sacrifice which witches and warlocks notoriously offered their Master?

The place could not be better chosen. This church was full, every one knew, of demons, who were certainly none other than the gods of the heathen, as Tertullian, Lactantius, Athenagoras, Justin Martyr, and all those other holy doctors had written. It was deserted, its keys in the hands of Cardinal Capranica's confidential architect and decorator; and there were masses being said every holiday to scare the evil spirits. The sacrament was frequently left on the altar.

All this Domenico expounded frequently to Filarete. But Filarete's classic taste did not approve of Domenico's methods, which savoured of vulgar witchcraft; perhaps also the learned man, who did not want the secret of antique proportion, recoiled from a degree of profanity and of danger, both to body and soul, which his companion willingly incurred in such a quest as his. So Filarete demurred for a time, until at length his feebler nature took fire at Dominico's determination, and the guilty pair fixed upon the day and place for this unspeakable sacrilege.

The Church of SS. Jervase and Protasius has undergone no change since the feast of Corpus Christi of the year 1488. The damp that lies in the atrium outside, making the grass and poppies sprout round the Byzantine pillar which carries a cross over a pine-cone, has invaded the flat-roofed nave and the wide aisles, separated from it by a single colonnade. A greenish mildew marks the fissures in the walls, rent here and there by landslips and earthquakes. The cipolline columns carrying the round arches on their square capitals are lustreless, and their green-veined marble looks like long-buried wood. The mosaic pavement stretches its discs and volutes of porphyry and serpentine or yellowed Parian marble, a tarnished and uneven carpet, to the greenish-white marble steps of the chancel. The mosaics have long fallen out of the circle of the apse; and the frescoes, painted by some obscure follower of Giotto, have left only a green vague stain over the arches of the aisle. Pictures or statues there are none, and no conspicuous sepulchre. Only, over the low entrance, a colossal wooden crucifix of the thirteenth century hangs at an angle from the wall, a painted Christ, stretching his writhing livid limbs in agony opposite the high altar. It was in this stately and desolate church, under the misty light that pours in through the wide windows of grey coarse glass, and on the marble altar facing that effigy of the dying Saviour, that, in derision as it were of the miracle which the church commemorates on that feast-day, Domenico and Filarete were about to offer up to the demons Apollo, Bacchus, and Jove the freshly consecrated wafer, the very body and blood of Christ.

But an accomplice of theirs, a certain monk well versed in magic, whom they employed in sundry details of devil-raising, on the score that they were seeking treasure hidden in the church, had suddenly been seized with qualms of conscience. Instead of appearing at the appointed time alone, and bearing certain necessaries of his art, he kept them waiting a full hour, until they began their proceedings without his assistance. And even as Domenico was reaching his companion the ostensorium, which had remained on the altar after the morning's mass, the church was surrounded by the officers of the Podestà on horseback, and by a crowd of monks and priests, and rabble who had followed them. Of these persons, not a few affirmed in after years, that, as they arrived at the church door, they had heard sounds of flutes and timbrels, and mocking songs filling the place; and that the devil, dressed in skins and garlands like a wild man of the woods, had cleft the roof with his head, and disappeared with many blasphemous yells as they entered.

VII

In those last years of the fifteenth century, Rome was a city of the Middle Ages. The cupola of the Pantheon, the circular hulk of the Colosseum, and the twin columns of Trajan and Antoninus projected, like the fantastic antiquities of some fresco of Benozzo Gozzoli, above domeless church roofs, battlemented palace walls, and innumerable Gothic belfries and feudal towers. In the theatre of Marcellus rose the fortress of the Orsinis; against the tower whence Nero, as the legend ran, had watched the city burning, were clustered the fortifications of the Colonnas; and in every quarter the stern palaces of their respective partisans frowned with their rough-hewn fronts, their holes for barricade beams, and hooks for chains. The bridge of St. Angelo was covered with the shops of armourers, as the old bridge of more peaceful Florence with those of silversmiths. Walls and towers encircled the Leonine City where the Pope sat unquietly in the big battlemented donjon by the Sixtine Chapel; and in its midst was still old St. Peter's, half Lombard, half Byzantine. In Rome there was no industry, no order, no safety. Through its gates rushed raids of Colonnas and Orsinis, sold to or betrayed by the Popes, from their castles of Umbria or the Campagna to their castles in town; and their feuds meant battles also between the citizens who obeyed or thwarted them. Houses were sacked and burnt, and occasionally razed to the ground, for the ploughshare and the salt-sower to go over their site. A few years later, when Pope Borgia dredged the Tiber for the body of his son, the boatmen of Ripetta reported that so many bodies were thrown over every night that they no longer heeded such occurrences. And when, two centuries later, the Corsinis dug the foundations of their house on the Longara, there were discovered quantities of human bones in what had been the palace of Pope della Rovere's nephew. Meanwhile Ghirlandaio and Perugino were painting the walls of the Sixtine; Pinturicchio was designing the blue and gold allegorical ceilings of the library; Bramante building the Chancellor's palace, and the Pollaiolas and Mino da Fiesole carving the tombs in St. Peter's, while learned men translated Plato and imitated Horace.

Of this Rome there remains nowadays nothing, or next to nothing. Sometimes, indeed, looking up the green lichened sides of some mediæval tower, with its hooks for chains, and its holes for beams, a vague vision thereof rises in our mind. And in the presence of certain groups by Signorelli, representing murderous scuffles or supernatural destruction, we feel as if we had come in contact with the other reality of those times, the thing which serene art and literature and the love of antiquity have driven into the background. But the complete vision of the time and place, the certain knowledge of that Rome of Sixtus IV. and Innocent VIII., we can now no longer grasp, a dreadful phantom passing too rapidly across the centuries.

It is with this feeling of impotence in my attempt to follow the thoughts of an illiterate artist of the Renaissance, that I prefer to conclude this strange story of the quest after antique beauty and antique gods by quoting a page from one of the barbarous chroniclers of mediæval Rome. The entry in the continuation of Infessura's diary is headed "Pictor Sacrilegus":—

"On the 20th July of the year of salvation fourteen hundred and eighty-eight, there were placed for three days in a cage on high in the Campo dei Fiori, Messer Niccolò Filarete, Canon of Sancto Joanne; also Domenico, the Volterran, painter and architect to the magnificent Cardinal Ascanio, and Frate Garofalo of Valmontone, they having been discovered in the act of desecrating the Church of SS. Jervase and Protasius, and stealing for magic purposes the ostensorium and many gold chalices and reliquaries with precious stones; and it was Frate Garofalo who, being versed in witchcraft and treasure finding, was the accomplice of the above, and denounced them on the feast of Corpus Domini. And the twenty-third of the said month of July they were justiced, and in this manner. *Videlicet*, Filarete and Domenico, having been removed from the cage, were dragged on hurdles as far as the square of San Joanni, and Frate Garofalo went on an ass, all of them crowned with paper mitres. Frate Garofalo was hanged to the elm-tree of the square. Of Filarete and Domenico, the right hand was chopped off, after which they were burned in the said square. And their chopped off right hands were taken to the Capitol and nailed up above the gate, alongside of the She-wolf of metal. Laus Deo."

VALEDICTORY

I

WHILE gathering together the foregoing pages, written at different periods and in different phases of thought, the knowledge has grown on me that I was saying farewell to some of the ambitions and to most of the plans of my youth.

All writers start with the hope of solving a problem or establishing a formula, however fragmentary or humble; and many, the most fortunate, and probably the most useful, continue to work out their program, or at least to think that they do so. Life to them is but the framework for work; and that is why they manage to leave a fair amount of work behind them,—work for other workers to employ or to undo. But with some persons, life somehow gets the better of work, becomes, whether in the form of circumstance or of new problems, infinitely the stronger; and scatters work, tossing about such fragments as itself, in its irregular, irresistible fashion, has torn into insignificance, or (once in a blue moon!) shaped into more complete meaning.

As regards my own case, I began by believing I should be an historian and a philosopher, as most young people have done before me; then, coming in contact with the concrete miseries of others, called social and similar problems, I sought to apply some of my historical or philosophic lore (such as it was) to their removal; and finally, life having manifested itself as offering problems (unexpected occurrence!) not merely concerning the Past, nor even the abstract Present, but respecting my own comfort and discomfort, I have found myself at last wondering in what manner thoughts and impressions could make the world, the Past and Present, the near and the remote, more satisfying and useful to myself. Circumstances of various kinds, and particularly ill-health, have thus put me, although a writer, into the position of a reader; and have made me ask myself, as I collected these fragments of my former studies, what can the study of history, particularly of the history of art and of other manifestations of past conditions of soul, do for us in the present?

All knowledge is bound to be useful. Apart from this truism, I believe that all study of past conditions and activities will eventually result, if not in the better management of present conditions and activities (as all partisan historians have hoped, from Machiavelli to Macaulay), at all events in a greater familiarity with the various kinds of character expressed in historical events and in the way of looking at them; for even if we cannot learn to guide and employ such multifold forces as make, for instance, a French revolution, we may learn to use for the best the individual minds and temperaments of those who describe them: a Carlyle, a Michelet, a Taine, are natural forces also, which may serve or may damage us.

Moreover, I hold by the belief, expressed years ago, in my previous volume of Renaissance studies, to wit, that historical reading (and in historical I include the history of thoughts and feelings as much as of events and persons) is a useful exercise for our sympathies, bringing us wider and more wholesome notions of justice and charity. And I feel sure that other uses for historical studies could be pointed out by other persons, apart from the satisfaction they afford to those who pursue them, which, considered merely as so much spiritual gymnastics, or cricket, or football, or alpineering, is surely not to be despised.

But now, having dropped long since out of the ranks of those who study in order to benefit others, or even to benefit only themselves, I would say a few words about the advantage which mere readers, as distinguished from writers, may get from familiarity with the Past.

This advantage is that they may find in the Past not merely a fine field for solitary and useless delusions (though that also seems necessary), but an additional world for real companionship and congenial activity. Our individual activities and needs of this kind are innumerable, and of infinite delicate variety; and there is reason to suppose that the place in which our lot is cast does not necessarily fit them to perfection. For things in this world are very roughly averaged; and although averaging is a useful, rapid way of despatching business, it does undoubtedly waste a great deal which is too good for wasting. Hence, it seems to me, the need which many of us feel, which most of us would feel, if secured of food and shelter, of spending a portion of their life of the spirit in places and climates beyond that River Oceanus which bounds the land of the living.

As I write these words, I am conscious that this will strike many readers as the expression of a superfine and selfish dilettantism, arising no doubt from morbid lack of sympathy with the world into which Heaven has put us. What! become absentees from the poor, much troubled Present; turn your backs to Realities, become idle strollers in the Past? And why not, dear friends? why not recognise the need for a holiday? why not admit, just because work has to be done and loads to be borne, that we cannot grind and pant on without interruption? Nay, that the bearing of the load, the grinding of the work, is useless save to diminish the total grinding and panting on this earth. Moreover, I maintain that we have but a narrow conception of life if we confine it to the functions which are obviously practical, and a narrow conception of reality if we exclude from it the Past. And not because the Past has been, has actually existed outside some one, but because it may, and often does, actually exist within ourselves. The things in our mind, due to the mind's constitution and its relation with the universe, are, after all, realities; and realities to count with, as much as the tables and chairs, and hats and coats, and other things subject to gravitation outside it. It would seem, indeed, as if the chief outcome of the spiritualising philosophy which maintains the immaterial and independent quality of mind had been to make mind, the contents of our consciousness, ideas, images, and feelings, into something quite separate from this real material universe, and hence unworthy of practical consideration. But granted that mind is not a sort of independent and foreign entity, we must admit that what exists in it has a place in reality, and requires, like the rest of reality, to be dealt with. But to return to my thesis: that we require occasionally to live in the Past (and I shall go on to state that it may be a Past of our own making); Do we not require to travel in foreign parts which know us not, to sojourn for our welfare in cities where we can neither elect members nor exercise professions, but whence we bring back, not merely wider views, but sounder nerves, tempers more serene and elastic? Nor is this all. We think poorly of a man or woman who, besides practical cases for self or others, does not require to come in contact also with the tangible, breathable, visible, audible universe for its own sake; require to wander in fields and on moors, to steep in sunshine or be battered by winds, for the sake of a certain specific emotion of participation in, of closer union with, the universal.

Now the Past—the joys and sufferings of the men long dead, their efforts, ideals, emotions, nay, their very sensations and temperaments as registered in words or expressed in art, are but another side of the universe, of that universal life, to participate ever deeper in which is the condition of our strength and serenity, the imperious necessity of our ever giving, ever taking soul.

And so, for our greater nobility and happiness, we require, all of us, to live to some extent in the Past, as to live to some extent in what we significantly call *nature*. We require, as we require mountain air or sea scents, hayfields or wintry fallows, sun, storm, or rain, each individual according to individual subtle affinities, certain emotions, ideals, persons, or works of art from out of the Past. For one it will be Socrates; for another St. Francis; for every one something somewhat different, or at all events something differently conceived and differently felt: some portion of the universe in time, as of the universe in space, which answers in closest and most intimate way to the complexion and habits of that individual soul.

II

The satisfaction which it can bring to every individual soul: this is, therefore, one of the uses of the Past to the Present, and surely not one of the smallest. It is,

I venture to insist, the special, the essential use of all art and all poetry; any additional knowledge of Nature's proceedings, any additional discipline of thought and observation which may accrue in the study of art as an historic or psychological phenomenon being, after all, valuable eventually for the amount of such mere satisfaction of the spirit as that additional knowledge or additional discipline can conduce towards. Scientific results are important for the maintenance of life, doubtless; but the sense of satisfaction, whether simple or complex, high or low, is the sign that the processes we call life are being fulfilled and not thwarted; so, since satisfaction is no such contemptible thing, why not allow art to furnish it unmixed?

I am sure to be misunderstood. I do not in the least mean to imply that art can best be appreciated with the least trouble. The mere fact that the pleasure of a faculty is proportioned to its activity negatives that; and the fact that the richness, fulness, and hence also the durability, of all artistic pleasure answers to the amount of our attention: the mine, the ore, will yield, other things equal, according as we dig, and wash, and smelt, and separate to the last possibility of separation what we want from what we do not want.

The historic or psychological study of art does thus undoubtedly increase our familiarity, and hence our enjoyment. The mere scientific inquiry into the difference between originals and copies, into the connection

Q

between master and pupil, makes us alive to the special qualities which can delight us. As long as we looked in a manner so slovenly that a spurious Botticelli could pass for a genuine one, we could evidently never benefit by the special quality, the additional excellence of Botticelli's own work. And similarly in the case of archæology. Indeed, in the few cases where I have myself hazarded an hypothesis on some point of artistic history, as, for instance, regarding the respective origin of antique and mediæval sculpture, I am inclined to think that the chief use (if any at all) of my work, will be to make my readers more sensitive to the specific pleasure they may get from Praxiteles or from Mino da Fiesole, than they could have been when the works of both were so little understood as to be judged by one another's standards.

But to return. It seems as if at present the development, the contagion, so to speak, of scientific methods applied to art were making people forget a little that art, besides being, like everything else, the passive object of scientific treatment, is (what most other things are not) an active, positive, special factor of pleasure; and that, therefore, save to special students, the greater, more efficacious form of art should occupy an immensely larger share of attention than the lesser and more inefficient. We are made, nowadays, to look at too much mediocre art on the score of its historical value; we are kept too long in contemplation of pictures and statues which cannot give much pleasure, on the score that they led to or proceeded from other pictures or statues which can.

As regards Greek sculpture, the insistance on archaic forms is becoming, if I may express my own feelings, a perfect bore. Why should we be kept in the kitchen tasting half-cooked stuff out of ladles, when most of us have barely time to eat our fully cooked dinner, which we like and thrive on, in peace? Similarly with such painters as are mainly precursors. They are taking up too much of our attention; and one might sometimes be tempted to think that the only use of great artists, like the only functions of those patriarchs who kept begetting one another, was to produce other great artists: Giotto to produce eventually Masaccio, Masaccio through various generations Michelangelo and Raphael, and Michelangelo and Raphael, through even more, Manet and Degas, who in their turn doubtless dutifully. . . . Meanwhile why should art have gone on evolving, artists gone on making *filiations of schools*, if art, if artists, if schools of artists had not answered an imperious, undying wish for the special pleasures which painting can give?

Therefore it seems to me that, desirable for all reasons as may be the study of art, the knowledge of *filiations and influences*, it is still more desirable that each of us should find out some painter whom he can care for individually; and that all of us should find out certain painters who can, almost infallibly, give immense pleasure to all of us; painters who, had they been produced out of nothingness and been followed by nobody, would yet stand in the most important relation in which an artist can be: the relation of being beloved by the whole world, or even by a few solitary individuals.

For this reason let not the mere reader, who comes to art not for work, but for refreshment, let not the mere reader (I call him reader, to note his passive, leisurely character) be vexed with too much study of Florentine and Paduan *precursors*, but go straight to the masters, whom those useful and dreary persons rendered possible by their grinding. Our ancestors, or rather those cardinals and superb lords with whom we have neither spiritual nor temporal relationship, who made the great collections of the seventeenth and eighteenth centuries, placing statues under delicate colonnades and green ilex hedges, and hanging pictures in oak-panelled corridors and tapestried guard-rooms, were occasionally mistaken in thinking that a Roman emperor much restored, or a chalky, sprawling Guido Reni, could afford lasting æsthetic pleasure; but, bating such errors, were they not nearer good sense than we moderns, who arrange pictures and statues as we might minerals or herbs in a museum, and who, for instance, insist that poor tired people, longing for a little beauty, should carefully examine the works of Castagno, of Rosselli, and of that artist, so interesting as a specimen of the minimum of talent, Neri di Bicci? They were unscientific, those lords and cardinals, and desperately pleasure-seeking; but surely, surely they were more sensible than we.

Connected with this fact, and to be borne in mind by those not called upon to elucidate art scientifically, is the further fact, which I have analogically pointed out, when I said that every individual has in the Past affinities, possibilities of spiritual satisfaction differing somewhat from those of every other. It is well that we should try to enlarge those possibilities; and we must never make up our mind that a picture, statue, piece of music or poetry, says little to us until we have listened to its say. But although we strive to make new friends, let us waste no further time on such persons as we have vainly tried to make friends of; and let each of us, in heaven's name, cherish to the utmost his natural affinities. There are persons to whom, for instance, Botticelli can never be what he truly is to some of their neighbours: the very quality which gives such marvellous poignancy of pleasure to certain temperaments causing almost discomfort to others; and similarly about many other artists, representing very special conditions of being, and appealing to special conditions in consequence. High Alpine air, sea-water, Roman melting westerly winds, so vitalising, so soothing to some folk, are mere worry, or fever, or lassitude to others, without its being correct to say that one set of persons is healthy and the other morbid: each being, in truth, healthy or morbid just in proportion as it realises its necessities of existence, fitting equally into the universe providing it be fitted each into the proper piece thereof.

On the other hand (and this, rather than *filiations of schools* and *influences* of artistic *milieus*, it were well we should know), it becomes daily more empirically certain, and will some day doubtless become scientifically obvious, that there are works of art which awaken such emotion that they can be delectable only to creatures with instincts out of gear and perception upside down; while there are others, infinitely more plentiful, which, in greater or lesser degree, must delight all persons who are sane, as all such are delighted by fine weather, normal exercise, and kindly sympathy; and, *vice versâ*, that as these wholesome works of art merely bore or actually distress the poor morbid exceptions, so the unwholesome ones sicken or harrow the sound generality ; the world of art, moreover, like every other world, being best employed in keeping alive its sound, not its unsound, clients.

Such works of art, such artists of widest wholesome appealingness, there are in all periods of artistic development; more in certain fortunate moments, say the Periklean age and the early sixteenth century, than in others; and most perhaps in certain specially favoured regions—in Attica during Antiquity, and during painting times, in the happy Venetian country. These we all know of; but by the grace of Nature, which creates men occasionally so fortunately balanced that their work, learned or unlearned, must needs be fortunately balanced also, they arise sometimes in the midst of mere artistic worry and vexation of spirit, or of artist bleakness, perfect like the almond and peach trees, which blossom, white and pink, on the frost-bitten green among the sapless vines of wintry Tuscan hills; and to some natures, doubtless, these are more pleasant and health-giving than more mature or mellow summer or autumnal loveliness. But, as I have said, each must find his own closest affinities in art and history as in friendship.

III

There are some more things, and more important, still to be said, from the reader's standpoint rather than the writer's, about the influence on our lives of the Past and of its art, and more particularly of the vague period called the Renaissance.

When the Renaissance began to attract attention, some twenty or twenty-five years ago, there happened among English historians and writers on art, and among their readers, something very similar to what had happened, apparently, when the Englishmen of the sixteenth century first came in contact with the Italian Renaissance itself, or whatever remained of it. Their conscience was sickened, their imagination hag-ridden, by the discovery of so much beauty united to so much corruption; and, among our latter-day students of the Renaissance, there became manifest the same morbid pre-occupation, the same exaggerated repulsion, which is but inverted attraction, which were rife among the playwrights who wrote of *Avengers* and *Atheists*, Giovannis and Annabellas, Brachianos and Corombonas, and other *White Devils*, as old Webster picturesquely put it, *of Italy*. Indeed, the second discovery of the Renaissance by Englishmen had spiritual consequences so similar to those of the first, that in an essay written fifteen years ago I analysed the feelings of the Elizabethan playwrights towards Italian things in order to vent the intense discomfort of spirit which I shared assuredly with students older and more competent than myself.

This kind of feeling has passed away among writers, together with much of the fascination of the Renaissance itself. But it has left, I see, vague traces in the mind of readers, rendering the Renaissance a little distasteful (and no wonder) to the majority; or worse, a little too congenial to an unsound minority; worst of all, tarnishing a little the fair fame of Art; and as a writer now turned reader, I am anxious to deliver, to the best of my powers, other readers from this perhaps inevitable but false and unprofitable view of such matters.

The conscience of writers on history and art has long become quite comfortable about the Renaissance; and the Websterian or (in some cases John Fordian) phenomenon of twenty years ago been forgotten as a piece of childish morbidness. Does this mean that the conscience has become hardened, that evil has ceased to repel us, or that beauty has been accepted calmly as a pleasant and necessary, but somewhat immoral thing? Very far from it. Our conscience has become quieter, not because it has grown more callous, but because it has become more healthily sensitive, more perceptive of many sides, instead of only one side of life. For with experience and maturity there surely comes, to every one of us in his own walk of life, a growing, at length an intuitive sense that evil is a thing incidentally to fight, but not to think very much about, because if it is evil, it is in so far sporadic, deciduous, and eminently barren; while good, that is to say, soundness, harmony of feeling, thought, and action with themselves, with others' feeling, thought, and action, and with the great eternities, is organic, fruitful and useful, as well as delightful to contemplate. Hence that the evil of past ages should not concern us, save in so far as the understanding thereof may teach us to diminish the evil of the Present. In any case, that evil must be handled not with terror, which enervates and subjects to contagion, but with the busy serenity of the physician, who studies disease for the sake of health, and eats his wholesome food after washing his hands, confident in the ultimate wholesomeness of nature.

And in such frame of mind the corruption of the Renaissance leaves us calm, and we know we had better turn our backs on it, and get from the Renaissance only what was good. Only, if we are physicians, or more correctly (since in a private capacity we all are) only *when* we are physicians, must we handle the unwholesome. Meanwhile, if we wish to be sound, let us fill our soul with images and emotions of good; we shall tackle evil, when need be, only the better. And here, by the way, let me open a parenthesis to say that, of the good we moderns may get from occasional journeys into the Past, there is a fine example in our imaginary and emotional commerce with St. Francis and his joyous theology. For while other times, our own among them, have given us loftier morality and severer good sense, no period save that of St. Francis could have given us a blitheness of soul so vivifying and so cleansing. For the essence of his teaching, or rather the essence of his personality, was the trust that serenity and joyfulness must be incompatible with evil; that simple, spontaneous happiness is, even like the air and the sunshine in which his beloved brethren the birds flew about and sang, the most infallible antidote to evil, and the most sovereign disinfectant. And because we require such doctrine, such personal conviction, for the better living of our lives, we must, even as to better climates, journey forth occasionally into that distant Past of mediæval Italy; and as to the Ezzelinos, Borgias, and Riarios, and the foul-mouthed humanists, good heavens! why should we sicken ourselves with the thought of this long dead and done for abomination?

So much for the history of the Renaissance and the

good it can be to us. Now as to the art. That more organic mode of feeling and thinking which results in active maturity, from the ever-increasing connections between our individual soul and the surrounding world; that same intuition which told us that historic evil was no subject for contemplation, does also admonish us never to be suspicious of true beauty, of thoroughly delightful art. Nay, beauty and art in any case; for though beauty may be adulterated, and art enslaved to something not itself, be sure that the element of beauty, the activity of art, so far as they are themselves specific, are far above suspicion even in the most suspicious company. For even if beauty is united to perverse fashions, and art (as with Baudelaire and the decadents) employed to adorn the sentiments of maniacs and gaol-birds, the beauty and the art remain sound; and if we must needs put them behind us, on account of too inextricable a fusion, we should remember it is as we sometimes throw away noble ore, for lack of skill to separate it from a base alloy. As regards the nightmare anomaly of perfect art arisen in times of moral corruption, those unconscious analogies I have spoken of, and which perhaps are our most cogent reasons, have taught us that such anomalies are but nightmares and horrid delusions. For, taking the phenomenon historically, we shall see that although art has arisen in periods of stress and change, and therefore of moral anarchy, it has never arisen among the immoral classes nor to serve any immoral use: the apparent anomaly in the Renaissance, for instance, was not an anomaly, but a coincidence of contrary movements: a materially prosperous, intellectually innovating epoch, producing on the one hand moral anarchy, on the other artistic perfection, connected not as cause and effect, but as coincidence, the one being the drawback, the other the advantage, of that particular phase of being. The Malatestas and Borgias, of whom we have heard too much, did not employ Alberti and Pier della Francesca, Pinturicchio and Bramante, to satisfy their convict wickedness, but to satisfy their artistic taste, which, in so far, was perfectly sound, as various others among their faculties, their eye and ear, and sense of cause and effect, were apparently sound also. And the architecture of Alberti, the decorations of Pinturicchio, remain as spotless of all contact with their evil instincts as the hills they may have looked at, the sea they may have listened to, the eternal verity that two and two make four, which had doubtless passed through their otherwise badly inhabited minds. And, moreover, the sea is still sonorous, the mountains are still hyacinth blue, and the buildings and frescoes still noble, while the rest of those disagreeable mortals' cravings and strivings are gone, and on the whole were best forgotten.

But there is another side of this same question, and of it we are admonished, as it seems to me, still louder by our growing intellectual instincts—those instincts, let us remember, which do but represent whatever has been congruous and uniform in repeated experience. Art is a much greater and more cosmic thing than the mere expression of man's thoughts or opinions on any one subject, of man's attitude towards his neighbour or towards his country, much as all this concerns us. Art is the expression of man's life, of his mode of being, of his relations with the universe, since it is, in fact, man's inarticulate answer to the universe's unspoken message. Hence it represents not the details of his existence, which, more's the pity, are rarely what they should be, whether in thought or action, but the bulk of his existence, *when that bulk is unusually sound*. This clause contains the whole philosophy of art. For art is the outcome of a surplus of human energy, the expression of a state of vital harmony, striving for and partly realising a yet greater energy, a more complete harmony in one sphere or another of man's relations with the universe. Now if evil is a non-vital, deciduous, and sterile phenomenon *par excellence*, art must be necessarily opposed to it, and opposed in proportion to art's vigour. While, on the other hand, the seeking, the realisation of greater harmony, whether harmony visible, audible, thinkable, and livable, is as necessarily opposed to anomaly and perversity as the great healthinesses of air and sunshine are opposed to bodily disease. Hence, in whatever company we find art, even as in whatever company we find bodily health and vigour, let us understand that *in so far as truly art*, it is good and a source of good. Let us never waver in our faith in art, for in so doing we should be losing (what, alas! Puritan contemners of art, and decadent defilers thereof, are equally doing) much of our faith in nature and much of our faith in man. For art is the expression of the harmonies of nature, conceived and incubated by the harmonious instincts of man.

I have given the influence of St. Francis as an example of what added strength our modern soul may get by a sojourn in the Past. What our soul may get of similar but more sober joy may be shown by another example from that wonderful Umbrian district, one of the earth's oases of spiritual rest and refreshment. Among all the sane and satisfying art of the Renaissance, Umbria, on the whole, has surely grown for us the highest and the holiest. I am not speaking of the fact that Perugino painted saints in devout contemplation, nor of their type of face and expression. Whatever his people might be doing, or if they were not people at all, but variations only of his little slender trees or distant domes and steeples, his art would have been equally high and holy. And this because of its effect, direct, unreasoning, on our spirit, making us, while we look, live with a deeper, more devoutly joyful life. What the man Perugino was, in his finite dealings with his clients and neighbours, has mattered nothing in the painting of these pictures and frescoes; still less what samples of conduct he was shown by the ephemeral magnificos who bought his works.

The tenderness and strength of the mediæval Italian temper (as shown in Dante when he is human, but above all in Francis of Assisi) has been working through generations toward these paintings, interpreting in its spirit, selecting and emphasising for its meaning the country in all the world most naturally fit to express it; and thus in these paintings we have the incomparable visible manifestation of a perfect mood: that wide pale shimmering valley, circular like a temple, and domed by the circular vault of sky, really turned, for our feelings, into a spiritual church, wherein not merely saints meditate and Madonnas kneel, but ourselves in deepest devout happiness.

IV

Thoughts such as these bring with them the memory of the master we have recently lost, of the master who, in the midst of æsthetical anarchy, taught us once more, and with subtle and solemn efficacy, the old Platonic and Goethian doctrine of the affinity between artistic beauty and human worthiness.

The spiritual evolution of the late Walter Pater—with whose name I am proud to conclude my second, as with it I began my first book on Renaissance matters—had been significantly similar to that of his own Marius. He began as an æsthete, and ended as a moralist. By faithful and self-restraining cultivation of the sense of harmony, he appears to have risen from the perception of visible beauty to the knowledge of beauty of the spiritual kind, both being expressions of the same perfect fittingness to an ever more intense and various and congruous life.

Such an evolution, which is, in the highest meaning, an æsthetic phenomenon in itself, required a wonderful spiritual endowment and an unflinchingly discriminating habit. For Walter Pater started by being above all a writer, and an æsthete in the very narrow sense of twenty years ago: an æsthete of the school of Mr. Swinburne's *Essays*, and of the type still common on the Continent. The cultivation of sensations, vivid sensations, no matter whether healthful or unhealthful, which that school commended, was, after all, but a theoretic and probably unconscious disguise for the cultivation of something to be said in a new way, which is the danger of all persons who regard literature as an end, and not as a means, feeling in order that they may write, instead of writing because they feel. And of this Mr. Pater's first and famous book was a very clear proof. Exquisite in technical quality, in rare perception and subtle suggestion, it left, like all similar books, a sense of caducity and barrenness, due to the intuition of all sane persons that only an active synthesis of preferences and repulsions, what we imply in the terms *character* and *moral*, can have real importance in life, affinity with life—be, in short, vital; and that the yielding to, nay, the seeking for, variety and poignancy of experience, must result in a crumbling away of all such possible unity and efficiency of living. But even as we find in the earliest works of a painter, despite the predominance of his master's style, indications already of what will expand into a totally different personality, so even in this earliest book, examined retrospectively, it is easy to find the characteristic germs of what will develop, extrude all foreign admixture, knit together congruous qualities, and give us presently the highly personal synthesis of *Marius* and the *Studies on Plato*.

These characteristic germs may be defined, I think, as the recurrence of impressions and images connected with physical sanity and daintiness; of aspiration after orderliness, congruity, and one might almost say *hierarchy;* moreover, a certain exclusiveness, which is not the contempt of the craftsman for the *bourgeois*, but the aversion of the priest for the profane uninitiated. Some day, perhaps, a more scientific study of æsthetic phenomena will explain the connection which we all feel between physical sanity and purity and the moral qualities called by the same names; but even nowadays it might have been prophesied that the man who harped upon the clearness and livingness of water, upon the delicate bracingness of air, who experienced so passionate a preference for the whole gamut, the whole palette, of spring, of temperate climates and of youth and childhood; a person who felt existence in the terms of its delicate vigour and its restorative austerity, was bound to become, like

Plato, a teacher of self-discipline and self-harmony. Indeed, who can tell whether the teachings of Mr. Pater's maturity—the insistance on scrupulously disciplined activity, on cleanness and clearness of thought and feeling, on the harmony attainable only through moderation, the intensity attainable only through effort—who can tell whether this abstract part of his doctrine would affect, as it does, all kindred spirits if the mood had not been prepared by some of those descriptions of visible scenes — the spring morning above the Catacombs, the Valley of Sparta, the paternal house of Marius, and that temple of Æsculapius with its shining rhythmical waters—which attune our whole being, like the music of the Lady in *Comus*, to modes of *sober certainty of waking bliss?*

This inborn affinity for refined wholesomeness made Mr. Pater the natural exponent of the highest æsthetic doctrine—the search for harmony throughout all orders of existence. It gave the nucleus of what was his soul's synthesis, his system (as Emerson puts it) of rejection and acceptance. Supreme craftsman as he was, it protected him from the craftsman's delusion —rife under the inappropriate name of "art for art's sake" in these uninstinctive, over-dextrous days—that subtle treatment can dignify all subjects equally, and that expression, irrespective of the foregoing *impression* in the artist and the subsequent *impression* in the audience, is the aim of art. Standing as he did, as all the greatest artists and thinkers (and he was both) do, in a definite, inevitable relation to the universe — the equation between himself and it — he was utterly unable to turn his powers of perception and expression to idle and irresponsible exercises; and his conception of art, being the outcome of his whole personal mode of existence, was inevitably one of art, not for art's sake, but of art for the sake of life — art as one of the harmonious functions of existence.

Harmonious, and in a sense harmonising. For, as I have said, he rose from the conception of physical health and congruity to the conception of health and congruity in matters of the spirit; the very thirst for healthiness, which means congruity, and congruity which implies health, forming the vital and ever-expanding connection between the two orders of phenomena. Two orders, did I say? Surely to the intuition of this artist and thinker, the fundamental unity — the unity between man's relations with external nature, with his own thoughts and with others' feelings — stood revealed as the secret of the highest æsthetics.

This which we guess at as the completion of Walter Pater's message, alas! must remain for ever a matter of surmise. The completion, the rounding of his doctrine, can take place only in the grateful appreciation of his readers. We have been left with unfinished systems, fragmentary, sometimes enigmatic, utterances. Let us meditate their wisdom and vibrate with their beauty; and, in the words of the prayer of Socrates to the

Nymphs and to Pan, ask for beauty in the inward soul, and congruity between the inner and the outer man; and reflect in such manner the gifts of great art and of great thought in our soul's depths. For art and thought arise from life; and to life, as principle of harmony, they must return.

Many years ago, in the fulness of youth and ambition, I was allowed, by him whom I already reverenced as a master, to write the name of Walter Pater on the flyleaf of a book which embodied my beliefs and hopes as a writer. And now, seeing books from the point of view of the reader, I can find no fitter ending to this present volume than to express what all we readers have gained, and lost, alas! in this great master.

THE END

Printed by BALLANTYNE, HANSON & CO.
Edinburgh and London

www.ingramcontent.com/pod-product-compliance
Lightning Source LLC
Chambersburg PA
CBHW031959230426
43672CB00010B/2202